D
Relia

MW01129484
(Sʀᴇ) Handbook

(2ⁿᵈ Edition)

Non Programmer's Guide

2 Manuscript Bundle

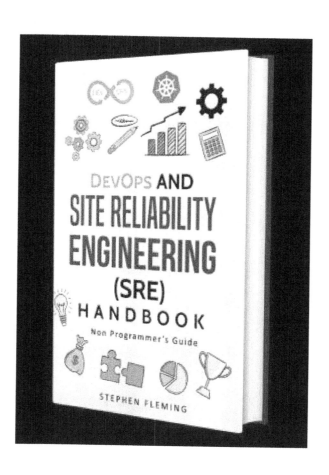

DevOps AND
SITE RELIABILITY
ENGINEERING
(SRE)
HANDBOOK

Non Programmer's Guide

STEPHEN FLEMING

2 Manuscript Bundle

5

Book 1: DevOps Engineer's Career Guide

6

7

Book 1:
The DevOps Engineer's Career Guide

A Handbook for Entry- Level Professionals to get into Continuous Delivery Roles for Agile Software Development

BONUS DEVOPS BOOKLET

Dear Friend,

I am privileged to have you onboard. You have shown faith in me and I would like to reciprocate it by offering the maximum value with an amazing gift. I have been researching on the topic and have an excellent "DevOps Booklet" for you to take your own expedition on DevOps to the next level.

- Do you want to know the job requirement of DevOps Engineer?
- Do you want to know the statistics of DevOps job available and mean salary offered?
- What are the latest trends in DevOps methodology
- People to follow on the latest on DevOps development

Also, do you want once in a while updates on interesting implementation of latest Technology; especially those impacting lives of common people?

"Get Instant Access to Free Booklet and Future Updates"

- Link: http://eepurl.com/dge23r

- QR Code: You can download a QR code reader app on your mobile and open the link by scanning below:

Preface

Hello! How are you and how is your Continuous Delivery journey going on? Are there any new skills that you want to acquire this year? If you do, please let me know what they are on my email.

My earlier books were on the following topics: DevOps, Microservices, and Kubernetes & Site Reliability Engineering.

In the last four months, I have been heavily involved in the recruitment process of various DevOps related jobs in my current project. I have come across multiple Entry Level and Mid-Level career professionals inquisitive about expectations of the role and how their earlier experience would contribute to the DevOps role. Also, I have received several emails from readers asking how to switch from their existing roles (development, sys admin, etc.). Based on the interactions, I have included "DevOps Engineer" related queries in the below categories and in this book, I will give you complete information about the position, career path and skill set required.

The main queries were the following:

- *Why DevOps?*

- *What are the job duties and day-to-day activities of a DevOps Engineer?*

- *What did DevOps engineers do before DevOps?*

- *What technical and soft skills are required to be an expert-level DevOps Engineer?*

- *What are some standard tools a DevOps engineer uses?*

- *What are other similar roles from where one can make the transition to the DevOps world?*

- *What are the Certifications/Courses one can do to become a DevOps Engineer?*

- *How can I get DevOps interviews with top companies?*

- *What are the average Salary, companies to work for, and designations/roles?*

- *How is the career path of a "DevOps Engineer"? How is the career advancement of a DevOps engineer?*

The book covers most of this information. Over the course of the book, you will gather information on what DevOps is, and how you can use it to improve your processes. You will also identify the different roles that are linked to DevOps. If you are keen on becoming a DevOps engineer, the last few chapters include information on what skills you need to develop and what path you need to choose. Also, the last chapter contains sample interview questions, which are the most common ones asked during a DevOps interview.

Overall, this book is aimed at professionals (0-5 years of experience) looking for a DevOps role overview in a limited timeframe. If you have to connect the dots regarding your existing experience, credentials and its fitment/relationship with the DevOps role, it would provide you with much-needed clarity. It also talks about other similar and related roles and its relationship with the DevOps role. Also, if you are part of the Project Management Team or Business Development Team or recruitment team (HR) this book will provide you required information about the DevOps role.

Thank you for purchasing the book. I hope that you get all the information you are looking for.

Chapter One
| An Introduction to DevOps |

DevOps is a collection of numerous concepts that are not entirely new. The concepts and techniques have created a change in the technical community and have spread across numerous projects. Since this term is not very popular, many people have confused its meaning and have the wrong impression of DevOps. This chapter will define DevOps by discussing its standard framework and the numerous areas that it covers. Like "Agile" and "Quality," DevOps is a concept that takes some time for an amateur to grasp. We will cover the basics of Agile in the third chapter of the book.

Definition of DevOps

A new abbreviation or term called DevOps was developed with the blending of two significant trends. The first of these trends is called agile infrastructure or agile operations, which sprung from the application of the Agile and Lean approaches to projects. The second trend is a deeper understanding of the collaboration between the development and operations staff when creating or operating service, through every stage of the process. DevOps also takes into account how essential operations have become for any business, as every industry is now customer-centric and service-oriented.

Jez Humble defined DevOps as a practice that uses information from different disciplines to study systems. The concept of DevOps is the study of the development and operation of rapidly changing systems. This is a good definition of DevOps, but for a startup or small company, it is too complicated. It would be best to define DevOps as a practice of development and operations engineers working together during the lifecycle of a process, including the development of the product and customer support. DevOps also has some techniques that both the operations and development staff use to make the systems work. These techniques range from participating in Agile development processes to using tools to test the process.

That's why there is no differentiation between different sub-disciplines in administration. The term "Ops" includes system administrators, system engineers, operations staff, release engineers, network engineers, DBAs, security professionals, ethical hackers and other job titles and sub-disciplines. The term "Dev" is an abbreviation of the term Developers, but it means so much more than that. The term "Dev" is a blanket term for all the employees or staff who are involved in the development of a product. These employees include Quality Analysts, Product Analysts and other employees from different disciplines.

DevOps is closely related to the Lean and Agile approaches. Earlier, the operations always focused on improving productivity and the end product. Not many businesses realized that this approach does not benefit the company and leads to further disarray within the firm. To overcome this, DevOps was created. You can look at DevOps as a branch of the Agile software. The Agile software development tool looks at how the product management team, developers, quality analysts, and customers collaborate to develop a better product. DevOps agrees that this collaboration is necessary, but it also states that the firm should provide the clients or customers with information about the service delivery and how the system and applications interact with one another. This means that the product management team must make this a high priority. If you look at it from this perspective, DevOps refers to extending the principles of Agile beyond the boundaries of simply setting the application up to the entire service the team needs to deliver.

Since the discussion around DevOps covers a lot of ground, people define DevOps in many different ways, since it means different things to them. Some people say that DevOps allows the team to treat the code as infrastructure, improves the collaboration between the operations team and development team, automates processes, improves culture, or is simply an alternative to Kanban. The only way one can define DevOps is by defining the term agile development. According to Wikipedia and the agile manifesto, Agile development includes four important factors. To define DevOps, I have included a fifth level called the tooling level. Most people do not like to talk about tools within the Agile and DevOps framework, but it is also difficult to ignore them.

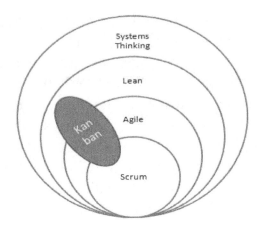

Agile Scrum & Kanban

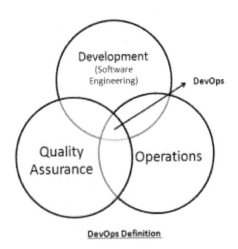

DevOps Definition

Agile Values

Agile values, which are included in the Agile Manifesto, are core values that have to be agreed upon. In the following chapter, we will shed some more light on these values.

Agile Principles

Agile Principles are the strategic approaches that support agile values. The Agile Manifesto cites many specific principles which are listed in the next chapter. You do not have to use all these principles, but if you do not abide by some of them, you will not be applying Agile to your process.

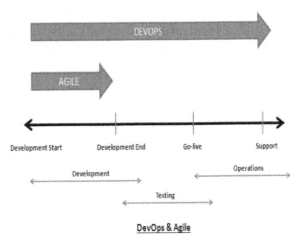

DevOps & Agile

Agile Methods

There are more specific processes to implement agile principles, which can be done with tools like Scrum and XP. Remember, none of these methods is mandatory, they're just possible ways to implement these principles.

Agile Practices

Agile practices are highly specific tactical techniques that are used along with Agile implementations. These practices do not have to be Agile, but by adopting these practices, you can increase the value of Agile implementations. These include planning poker, standups, backlog and other artefacts that a developer will use to perform their work.

Agile Tools

In order to improve their work, some teams use tools like planningpoker.com, Greenhopper and other Agile tools to implement Agile practices.

Agile uses a top-down approach where the higher levels inform the lower levels. If an organization or a team pick up tools and practices without fully understanding the fundamentals, they cannot reap the benefits. This is because, in the past, this approach has never worked. People always talk about DevOps in parts, but all the parts will map to the principles and values of DevOps.

DevOps Values

The fundamental values of DevOps can be found in the Agile Manifesto.

However, instead of only making it a working software, there is a slight change to focus on the overall software or service that is delivered to the customer. Alex Honor defined DevOps as 'People over Processes over Tools.' The DevOps values echo the Agile values and urge the collaboration between the development and operations team.

DevOps Principles

There is no single list of principles, but some of the widely accepted ones are covered in Chapter Three. One of the universal principles of DevOps is "infrastructure as code." Experts believe that DevOps is a branch of the Agile principles since it also includes the collaboration between systems and operations, and does not only stop at checking the code.

DevOps Methods

You can use Kanban, Scrum, and other Agile methods for operations. The focus is on integrating the operations with the development, quality analyst and product teams. There are also other distinct methods like Incident Command Systems and Visible Ops. The former works towards changing control within the team while the latter works on recording any incidents. A combination of these methodologies is growing, and experts are trying to develop a more thoughtful process to monitor them.

DevOps Practices

There are specific techniques that you can use to implement the above processes and concepts. Configuration management, continuous integrations, continuous deployment, toolchain approach to tooling, monitoring and metrics schemes and cloud computing and visualization are some of the standard practices that one uses to bring change using DevOps.

DevOps Tools

The DevOps Tools are tools you will use to commission the principles. Recently, many tools have been released in the

DevOps world. The following are some of the ones developed for different departments:

- To monitor releases – Jenkins, TeamCity, Travis

- For configuration management – Chef, Puppet, Cfengine, Ansible

- For orchestration – Noah, Mesos, Zookeeper

- For containerization, monitoring and visualization – AWS, Vagrant, Docker, and OpenStack

It is incorrect to call any tool a DevOps tool as it will not magically help you follow the principles and values of DevOps. Some specific tools are being developed to facilitate the implementation of the principles, practices, and methods of DevOps thereby helping you develop a holistic understanding of DevOps.

It is difficult to define DevOps, just like it is difficult to define Agile, but it is worth doing. When you look at the definition on a philosophical level, it can seem like an empty statement. Some people may wonder why they are being asked to do their jobs better. You must remember that just because you follow some instructions in a book, it does not mean that you are developing an Agile process. If you want to be a DevOps Engineer or an Agile practitioner, you must understand all the layers that go into making you an engineer, and how you can implement these tools and practices to help you develop a robust process. What DevOps wants to bring into Agile is the notion that the product or software is not fully developed until it meets the expectations of the users or customers.

When people talk about DevOps, three primary areas of practice that are often discussed are the following:

Infrastructure Automation

Here, you will need to create the systems, configure the operating system and use different application deployments as your code.

Continuous Delivery

In this practice, you need to build, test and deploy the application in an automated and speedy way.

Site Reliability Engineer

The site reliability engineer will operate the systems, monitor how they function and design the systems to allow collaboration between different teams.

History of DevOps

DevOps was developed when people and firms realized that they needed to innovate and automate processes on the technology side. The DevOps movement only started after the Enterprise Systems Management (ESM) and System Administration movement.

ESM rose in the 2000s, and it made people wonder what they could do to improve the processes. Companies and firms realized that their systems were still in the primitive state despite the effort that the employees put into improving the systems. Then, they began to look for different ways to improve these systems. John Willis, Mark Hinkle and Whurley from Zenoss sponsored a Barcamp around that concept.

In the year 2008, O'Reilly held the first Velocity conference which focused on the performance and operations of the internet. It allowed professionals from different fields to share information about the best practices for operations. In the year 2009, there were presentations about the advantages of collaboration between the development and operations team in large businesses. They also talked about how this collaboration promoted a rapid and safe change in web environments. Tools like Chef and Puppet were marketed the most, and people then began to wonder how they could use these new concepts and implement them in their organization.

In parallel, in the development space, Agile development processes began to grow in popularity. As most organizations were talking about Agile Systems Administration, Agile processes moved from being a niche practice to a more common one. This was especially true in Europe. Gordon Banner had addressed this in the early 2000s during a meet. Most of the focus of this movement was on the processes and the analogies from lean manufacturing processes and Kanban. In the year 2009, Patrick Debois and Andrew Clay Shafer sat down and talked about the collaboration between the development and operations teams and coined the term DevOps. Then, Patrick held a DevOps Days event in Ghent which lit the fuse. Now that the concept had a name, many people began to talk about it, and it was discussed in many events including Velocity.

In Patrick Debois' view, the concept of DevOps rose like a reaction against the inflexibilities and silos due to existing practices. This does sound familiar. To understand DevOps better, you should read more articles on the internet about the history of the movement.

Chapter Two:
| Facts and Benefits of DevOps |

Benefits of DevOps

Now that you have an idea what DevOps is, let's look at the benefits that a business can gain by deploying DevOps.

Quicker Deployment of New Applications and Systems

If you have successfully incorporated DevOps into your business, you should now work towards the next level of deployment. If you use the right approaches, you can ensure that your organization deploys its new systems in an enhanced and efficient manner. This can be done while maintaining and even sometimes maximizing efficiency. This is how continuous deployment and innovations become synonymous with each other. This makes it easier to deploy products and services faster.

Agility Is Key

It is essential for the business to be agile

for it to go through a transformation. Through DevOps, any organization, regardless of its size, can transform the business into a more Agile system, which will allow it to achieve scalability. In simpler words, everybody wins.

DevOps Directly Translates Into Money

Through DevOps, a business can automate repetitive tasks without worrying too much about any errors. For instance, performance and regression testing can quickly bring about small changes. Frequent rollovers and backups in the development chain will lead to a more stable and robust process. When you have such automation in place, the organization can benefit by saving a large chunk of its manual costs. This therefore directly translates to saving money.

With DevOps, Silos Can No Longer Exist

Silos and innovation are things of the past. In today's world of business, there is more to innovation than meets the eye. In the past, there was never a link between the operations and development team, which meant that any innovation was carried out in complete secrecy. This made it difficult for an organization to maintain transparency. Times have changed, and so have the methods of innovation processes. Since there is an increased level of interaction between different teams in the organization, there is now more exposure. This exposure enables transparency between teams which creates a useful collaboration. This change can be brought about by following Agile methodologies since they have given a new meaning to innovation, thereby making it easier for employees. In a typical IT organization, there are many barriers that one must break with the right approach. Through the introduction of DevOps, an organization can get rid of old linear processes and introduce new processes that will improve the functions of the company.

Faster Development Cycles for the Organization

Communication and collaboration are the two main keywords relating to DevOps. In an organization, when these features are enhanced, there is an instant improvement in development cycles. This helps the organization achieve success regardless of what the project may be.

Continuous Service Delivery

Through DevOps, the organization can ensure shorter development cycles. This means that after they go through a series of tests, the codes are quickly released to the end users. There is very little or no gap between gathering requirements and the production cycle, which helps to create a massive shift in a production cycle. Using these methods, the organization can synchronize IT mechanisms with production cycles, thereby streamlining the cycle. This helps to improve the efficiency of the process, and that's why an effective DevOps method should be incorporated

34

into the system to create a stable and robust method to check efficiency.

Adieu Defects

In every application production environment, defects are your worst enemy. When you incorporate DevOps methods into your processes, you can reduce the number of defects to zero, and that's why most organizations are now using DevOps methods to develop software. Through iterative development, modular programming and collaboration, teams can minimize any defects, thereby developing a foolproof method to handle or overcome defects. There are many alternative methods that the organization can use to minimize defects, which helps to increase efficiency in every aspect of the organization.

With so many benefits to using DevOps methods, people now believe that DevOps is the future of the production cycle. If it is implemented correctly, organizations can achieve a lot in a short period.

What is DevOps Not?

It's Not NoOps

Some people believe that DevOps means that the developer takes over the operations tasks. They worry that the developers are taking over their jobs. Not completely, but there is some truth to that.

It is a misconception that DevOps is a working method that begins from the development side that is used to wipe out operations. You must remember that DevOps, like Agile and other processes, is initiated by the operations team. This is because the operations team realized that the existing processes, principles, and practices do not help in developing successful projects. Since development teams and businesses need more agility, the business climate becomes more fast-paced. Since the climate is rapidly changing, we provide less to the end user since we are trying our best to solve problems with more rigidity. This means that we need a fundamental orientation to provide the teams with the necessary infrastructure.

It is only now that we realize that there are some parts of the operations process that we need to automate. This means that the operations team can work on automating processes, or it can be done by the developers by writing code to build new ones. There are times when both the developers and operations work together to build robust processes. This may seem scary to some people, but it is a part of the collaborative approach. Teams will be successful only when the development team and the operations team work together to create an overall product.

It's Not (Just) Tools

DevOps is not just the implementation of tools. It is essential to define DevOps since many people misunderstand the term, using a poorly structured definition that ignores the theory and implements the many tools and processes of DevOps without keeping the principles in mind. This is an antipattern. You must remember that automation is just one way to exercise power, and if you do not automate processes wisely, you will damage the system.

Agile practitioners will also tell you that you should never begin working in iterations and adopt other practices or tools without starting the collaboration, as it will damage the process and the software. Many teams in various companies only adopt some methods of Agile but never worry about its principles. The results of such processes are suboptimal. You can use a tool in Agile, but if you are unaware of how to use it, you will undoubtedly damage the process.

In the end, it is not about fretting about which tools you should use for DevOps. If you were to plan an Agile process, do you think it would magically happen? No, you will need to use different tools that adhere to the Agile values. The same can be said about DevOps, a system that works only when its values are kept in mind.

It's Not (Just) Culture

Most people insist that DevOps is a culture. They believe that one cannot apply that word to a principle or practice, but this is simply incorrect. Agile has helped many organizations and firms develop, but the development will reach a plateau since Agile stops at culture. This is because a lead practitioner in a team always decides what process the team should follow. They also refused to be more prescriptive. DevOps always contains rules or values for all the items in the list above. Since you will have enough time to experiment, you will be able to identify the best practices yourself, but it is always a good idea to fall back on some tried and tested policies before you start developing your own.

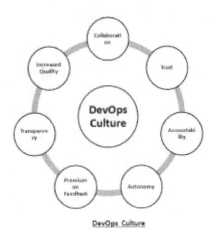

DevOps Culture

It's Not (Just) Developers and Operations

You must remember that it is not exclusionary. Some people claim that we don't care about network administrators, the security team and other smaller teams. The objective of DevOps is to create a system or product that can collaborate right from the start. This means that developers, operation teams, and business folk of various types need to work together to develop a strong process. These people include network administrators, security teams and every single other employee. There

40

are different types of developer and business stakeholders, and just because they are not personally called for a discussion, it does not mean that they are not involved.

When Agile was first developed, people only cared about the collaboration between the business and the development team. DevOps always looks at issues and solutions around the collaboration between the development and operations teams. The result of using DevOps in your company is that everyone collaborates to develop the perfect product. From this perspective, DevOps is a significant step that allows all disciplines within an organization to collaborate. Regardless of what role an employee or team play, if it does participate in the delivery of the software, it is a part of DevOps.

It's Not (Just) A Job Title

It does not make sense to take an existing operations team and rename it as a DevOps team. This does not help the situation at all, and it does not help to change the job title or role to DevOps Engineer. If you do not want to adopt any of the principles or values of DevOps, you will not reap any of the benefits since you will need to make changes to the overall system.

That does not mean that you cannot have a role that is called "DevOps Engineer." This title is often used to differentiate between the new style of thinking – where you first focus on automation, collaboration and the overall working of the software – from the old way of thinking where the person at the back-end does not necessarily care about what you do in your firm. Some people will find value in that, while others will not. If you are hiring a DevOps engineer, you should ensure that the applicant fits the role perfectly, and clearly know how they will work towards improving the process.

It's Not Everything

Sometimes, DevOps engineers get carried away and claim that this process regards every process everywhere.

DevOps does plug into the overall structure of the organization, and it does use the principles of Agile and Lean thinking. There are opportunities to collaborate and build better and more efficient processes in an organization. It is always nice to see how you can use different tools in parallel; however, DevOps is not necessarily going to re-engineer all the business and its processes.

DevOps is a part of an overall agile and collaborative corporate culture, but it also looks at how different operations can plug into that. Some folks try too hard and turn the complete process into a watered-down version of Agile or Lean. This is a great vision, but when you move down and look at the granular sections of the process, you will see that you are just dealing with operational integration. There will still be a lot of problems that are not being addressed, and these issues revolve around the service maintenance, delivery of software and software development.

To increase the scope of projects, it is fine to use the different DevOps tools. Most DevOps engineers, however, want to identify ways to improve their jobs rather than another person's. In Agile process management, there is Agile organization work and Agile Software Development. DevOps can be defined as an Agile Software Operations and Delivery process. This means that using DevOps, one should work on large organizational initiatives without losing sight of the primary values or objectives of the organization.

Getting Started With DevOps

You cannot follow a path to DevOps in your organization. All you need to do is look at different processes or tools that work for your organization. Most successful DevOps initiatives have originated from the collaboration of the development and operations teams, a bottom up and top down approach, from consultants and from inside the company, skunkworks pilots and widespread education. Therefore, it is always hard to follow steps to develop a process and implement it in your firm. It is safe to say that it always starts with the individuals in the organization. You will need to learn the values, principles, practices, and methods of DevOps and then try to spread that via an effective channel. This channel can be through the other members of the team, other employees in the company, and management. Alternatively, you can implement different strategies in the company by yourself and let the success speak for itself. People will always tell you how you can rise to success, but that advice is more wishful thinking and policy than reality. You should observe how some popular methods and tools rose in your organization, and try those channels. Always keep learning.

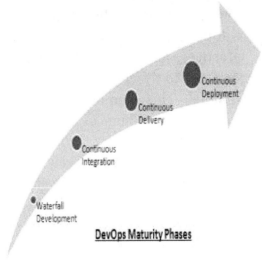

DevOps Maturity Phases

Continuous Deployment

Continuous Delivery

Continuous Integration

Waterfall Development

Chapter Three
|An Introduction to Agile Management|

To better understand DevOps, you should understand the different Agile techniques, as DevOps is an offshoot of it. Agile is an approach that adheres to twelve principles and the Agile Manifesto.

Pillars of Improvement

The Agile model is based on the following pillars, and DevOps and other Agile processes adhere to these principles.

Transparency

One feature of agile and DevOps is unfettered transparency. The information is passed from one member of the team to the next with ease. There are clear channels of communication. The organization will have a clear idea of what task each team is working on, and how many tasks are still in the product log. This is because the team works towards developing results right from the beginning of the cycle. Once the results or products hit the end users, feedback is sent to the team and improvements are made where necessary.

Transparency is not about viewing the results and quickly completing the work. Every member of the team should always look at the process through the same lens. The team should share a common framework and should collectively decide which task or requirement is a high priority. This will allow the organization and the team to know what the status of every requirement is.

Inspection

In the Agile framework, the tasks are broken down into smaller pieces of work. Every team is given a goal that it must achieve in a set period. This is called the sprint. When each

48

requirement (also called a feature or user story) is completed, the team will test that feature to ensure that it works well. The team must also consider the customer's requirements.

People who work closely with the project will always inspect the results. These people include the end user and the development teams. This will help to reduce the time lag, and it also means that any adjustments can be made to the feature immediately as the information is readily available.

Adaptation

If the team notices any inaccuracies or inefficiencies during the process, it should make changes to it immediately. This means that the team should learn to immediately adapt and make adjustments before it begins another task. In other words, teams should always understand which parts of the process are functioning well and which aren't. Through Agile and DevOps, the development and operations team have the right to inspect the work, thereby

49

allowing the team to work collectively towards improving the process.

The Agile Manifesto

Agile is a framework that one can follow, and it should not be thought of as a methodology or process. You will need to make some choices. The biggest advantage of using Agile is that you can make some decisions that are best for the team using the feedback that comes from your end users.

The following are the values that form the Agile Manifesto, and every organization that wants to use Agile or DevOps must adhere to these values:

- Individuals and interactions between those individuals will take precedence over processes and tools.

- A working software model is more important to develop, rather than comprehensive documentation.

- Always collaborate with end users

before a negotiation.

- Respond to change and adapt your process if necessary.

Although the Agile Manifesto and its principles were written by and for software, the values are valid for any project that your organization takes up. The GPS was initially designed for the military, but today, every individual in the world uses it to track someone or reach their destination. For more information on the history of the Agile Manifesto and its founders, visit http://agilemanifesto.org.

Agile Principles

The founders or developers of Agile did not just stop at writing the values. They also defined some principles that teams must follow to adhere to those values. You can incorporate these values into your project and assess whether the framework you have developed adheres to these values.

- You should always satisfy the

customer and deliver the software or product early and quickly. Alternatively, you can choose to deliver small sections of the product, called user stories or features to the customers.

- You should take customer feedback seriously and make changes to the product regardless of what stage the project is at. An agile process will allow you to make any change to the product if it improves customer satisfaction.

- Always deliver a working prototype of the software to the end user at regular intervals.

- Business or operations teams and development teams should always work together throughout the project.

- Ensure that the development team receives all the necessary support to ensure that the task is being done.

- Always have meetings where every team can convey information to other teams efficiently and effectively.

- Measure your progress by developing working prototypes of the product.

- Sponsors, users, and developers should always be on the same page throughout the project.

- Attention to detail and good design will improve the agility of the process.

- Following a simple process is important. This implies that you should identify ways to maximize the amount of work the team does not have to do.

- A self-organizing team can provide the best architecture and design.

- Teams should always reflect on what they should do to be more effective. They should then adjust their behaviour accordingly.

The principles of Agile will never change, but the tools that a team uses to adhere to those principles can change. It is easier to implement some principles over others. For example, if you look at the second principle, the team can be open to new ideas and change. For such teams, it is easy to develop a framework and work on tasks. On the other hand, there will be teams who are more resistant to change.

Take a look at the sixth principle. Today, it is difficult for most teams to work face-to-face on a project due to the globalization of the workforce. You may have teams sitting in India, the United States of America and Russia. Instead of thinking that the principle cannot be applied to your team, you should look for a solution. Can you use Skype to stay in touch with the different members of the team? This is not what the sixth principle says, but if you want to improve processes, you should focus on how to deal with the principle today. This means that you should always learn to adapt to change.

Every team will face unique challenges, and you should never let a hiccup stop you from working on the project. Part of the fun is to work through issues and achieve the desired results. The same can be said about all principles. You can improve your team's quality and efficiency if you adhere to the principles listed above.

Platinum Principles

Experts suggest that a team or organization should abide by these principles when working on a project as they help to improve efficiency, as well as assist in the implementation process.

Avoiding Formality

Have you ever sat through a presentation and wondered how the presenter made such an amazing presentation? Do you wonder how much time that person spent to develop it? When you think that you are only preparing a presentation for a project, you are wasting your time. You can scribble whatever you want to say on a small sheet of paper and then get back to doing what you need to do. If you are concerned about a task or anything, you should speak to the concerned party and ask them to help you with it. You should always try to focus on your objectives and not worry about how to prepare a presentation.

Atos Origin conducted a survey, and it concluded that an average employee spends at least forty per cent of his or her productive hours on emails that do not add any value to the project or business. This means that for that employee, the workweek begins on Wednesday. People often confuse themselves with pageantry and progress. In an Agile system, you are encouraged to communicate directly and informally when you have a question. This will help you save time because you will work closely with every other member of the team. You have to always identify a simple way to achieve your goals.

Your projects will evolve and abide by the Agile values in no time. When people are more aware of the process, they work towards developing a robust or stable system.

Think and Act as a Team

The objective of Agile is to ensure that teams work well together. It is difficult to bring teams and individuals together since most organizations pit an individual against his or her peers. Individuals are encouraged to compete with their peers and are always questioning what they can do better to succeed in that environment. In Agile, the project will either thrive or die at the team level. When teams work well together and leverage the talent of an individual for the benefit of that team, they become hyper-productive. Aristotle once said, 'The whole is greater than the sum of its parts,' and this holds true for teams.

So, how do you develop this type of culture? The Agile framework only emphasizes on teams. Common goals, collective ownership, and physical space will improve the dynamics of a team. You should then add the following to your framework:

- Get rid of all work titles. No employee owns the team or some areas of development. One should establish themselves through his or her contribution and skills.

- Report only team metrics, and never an individual or pairing metrics.

- Always pair team members to improve cross-functionality and improve the quality of work.

Visualize Instead of Writing

It is important to remember that people are visual. When they think pictorially, they will remember everything they have read about. Most children's books now have numerous images. As a kid, what did you like best about books? The text or the images? We are no different as adults. We will flip through a magazine to look at images, and if there is something that we like, we stop to read the article.

Diagrams, graphs, and pictures can relay information in an instant. If you write a huge report, people will stop reading because they know that there is no diagram to support any claim you are making. Twitter wanted to study the effectiveness of tweets without photos versus those with photos. It used SHIFT Media Manager to conduct this analysis, and it came up with some interesting results. A user would engage five times more frequently if a tweet included a photo. The rate of retweets for posts with photos were double those without. Also, they found that the cost per engagement of text-only tweets is double that of photo tweets.

You should always encourage your team to present information using visual aids, even if it means that they need to sketch a diagram on a whiteboard. If there is someone who does not understand the diagram, they can always ask you to explain. The same can be done with technology – you can either make models, charts or graphs to explain the technology.

Chapter Four
| DevOps Principles and Concepts |

DevOps Principles

Now that we have covered the Agile principles in the previous chapter, let's look at the most popular DevOps principles.

Customer Centric Action

It is essential to have short feedback loops where you directly communicate with end-users and real customers. You should also ensure that the activities that the team performs are only centred around these clients. If you want to meet your customer's requirements, you must act like a lean startup and always innovate your processes. If there is a strategy that is not working, you should have the guts to use a new one. You have to identify the products and services that delight your customers the most and invest in improving those products and services.

Always Create With The End In Mind

Every organization should now let go of the process-oriented and waterfall approach. In those approaches, an individual or a team works on a specific function or role without looking at the complete picture. Organizations should start acting like product companies and focus only on building working products. Employees should all share an engineering mindset, which will allow them to envision the final product.

End-To-End Responsibility

In traditional organizations, the development team will take care of developing IT solutions or products, and then hand those products over to the Operations team. The Operations team will then deploy those products to customers as well as maintain them. In DevOps, the teams are organized vertically, which means that every team in the organization is accountable. The products and services that are developed by these teams will always remain under their focus. These teams will also identify ways to support and improve performance, which will enhance the level of responsibility, thereby increasing the quality of products.

Cross-Functional Autonomous Teams

In most product organizations, the teams must be fully independent throughout the process or lifecycle of the product. This means that they need to balance the skills in the team. This also means that the members of the team should be well versed and have enough information regarding what the other teams are doing. These teams will grow rapidly and develop products that will meet user requirements. It's possible that the feedback loop becomes smaller as the teams know what needs to be done to meet the requirements.

Continuous Improvement

Organizations must continuously adapt to ensure that they incorporate the changing circumstances including a change in customer needs, technology, and legislation. In DevOps, a strong focus is always maintained on the continuous improvement of processes to increase speed, optimize costs, improve delivery and minimize waste. The organization should also focus on improving the products or services that it develops. Therefore, it is important for teams to experiment to ensure that they learn from their failures and develop robust processes. A rule to live by is to fail more to learn more.

Automate Everything

Organizations should work toward continuously improving their processes. To do this, the organization must get rid of some waste. In the last few years, many companies have identified a way to eliminate waste from different processes to improve the products and services that it deploys. As an organization, you should always think of ways to automate the software development process and the infrastructure landscape by building cloud platforms that will allow you to view the infrastructure as a program or code.

Key Concepts and Metrics

Focus On Deployment Lead Time

Deployment lead time is a part of the value stream, and it starts when an engineer in the value stream wants to change a version of the software. The time taken for the engineer to push the change into the software, run that change in production and obtain feedback from the customer regarding the change is calculated as the deployment time.

Instead of processing large batches of work in short periods, the goal is to test smaller batches of work. The goal is to test and operate the software while working on its design and development This will improve the quality of work and also enable the team to develop the software faster. That is why teams should break the project into smaller segments before they begin working on their development.

Process Time and Lead Time

In Lean, the lead time is one of the measures or criteria used to measure the performance of the team. The other measure is the processing time. The lead time begins when the customer makes a request, and it ends when the request is met. The processing time starts when the team begins to work on the customer's request. It does not consider the time when the work or process is in the job queue. Since the customer experiences lead time, we will focus on how to minimize it. Experts suggest that teams should look at the processing time and identify ways to reduce it.

Chapter Five
| Essential Skills for the DevOps Engineer |

What does a DevOps engineer do?

DevOps is a joint process between software development and IT operations. Large companies are increasingly relying on the concept of DevOps to deliver high-quality products at an increased pace. DevOps engineers enable effective communication between these two entities to improve software development and delivery, enabling the organization to better and more effectively serve clients. They also facilitate continuous integration and development of output generated by back-end teams, ensuring a good pipeline for delivery of the code. Due to the integration of two separate processes, DevOps does not have a formal definition. Instead, DevOps engineers are either software developers who exhibit proclivity towards the operations aspect of a business, or operations professionals who are passionate about writing code and script.

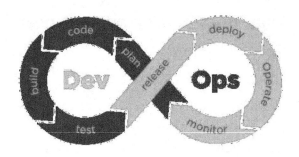

(https://medium.com/@neonrocket/de vops-is-a-culture-not-a-role-be1bed149b0)

Reflecting changes

It is difficult to track the changes in a traditional software development process. Changes in the code are possible but their reflection in a production environment is time-consuming, and this delays the release of the product. DevOps engineers can solve this by implementing a CI/CD pipelines to improve the speed of testing, development, and deployment.
68

Feedback and monitoring

Feedback loops developed for implementation, modification, and validation are time-consuming. Now that the delivery pipeline is automated and there is constant feedback from the client, monitoring projects across the organization becomes easy.

Frequent and reliable releases

Updates, releases and version controls such as waterfall, spiral or iterative are critical points in development models. These decelerate the market availability of your application despite only needing a small bug fix. DevOps engineers can solve this problem efficiently and quickly, as they tend to work with the tools and strategies that bridge the gap between 'development' and 'operation.'

What is a typical day in the life of a DevOps engineer?

The role of a DevOps engineer is centred on bridging product development and delivery while meeting the automation needs of other team members.

69

Therefore, a typical day in a DO engineer's life involves numerous meetings to ensure smooth inter-team collaboration and a focus on reducing overall manual effort.

How do I become a good DevOps engineer?

Successful DevOps engineers often possess most, if not all the skills listed below:

- The ability to collaborate effectively and skillfully

- The ability to facilitate seamless end-to-end communication

- Experience in development

- The ability to supervise infrastructure planning, testing, and development

- They ensure security and rapidity across the organization

- A clear understanding of DevOps tools, structure, processes and mindsets

- Anticipate needs, accumulate resources, and plan accordingly

- An eye to detect issues in automation, version control, and overall security and suggest necessary steps to solve them quickly

- Passion: At the end of the day, passion defines a good candidate, and it's an asset that cannot be replaced.

What are the skills needed to become a good DevOps engineer?

Although there is no formal career track to become a DevOps engineer, the processes of development and operations can be used to define the skills required to become an accomplished DevOps engineer. Mainly, these skills are the following:

Technical Proficiency

DevOps is a highly technical field. If

your background is in operations, begin sharpening your development skills with programming languages such as Python, Ruby, and Perl because you will be required to automate processes by writing code. Experience with scripting and administration platforms is also highly desirable to potential employers because server deployment is a significant bottleneck in the IT industry. Therefore, familiarize yourself with Linux and Ubuntu. On the other hand, if you are already a developer, learn how software delivery and deployment work. DevOps engineers must understand networking and storage because these are no longer silos. The need of the hour is to develop scalable solutions that function rapidly at any given time.

Automation Tools

As mentioned previously, the redundancy associated with many processes such as manual ones like assigning IP addresses and DNS reservation can be eliminated by scripts written in languages like Python and Ruby. Every DevOps role requires you to have some knowledge of deploying, operating and building software regardless of the type of stack used in the system. You must always be willing to apply the knowledge you have to use new tools whenever needed. Since most DevOps tools focus on automation, it is important that you familiarize yourself with different automation tools and techniques. This will improve performance and remove the human component, thereby allowing the team to save some time. A DevOps engineer must be able to implement automation technologies and tools at any level.

Puppet, Vagrant

It is critical to maintaining consistency in being available, as well as reliable and quick. Experience with these tools will help you repetitively and predictably manage software and system alterations.

Jenkins, Maven

Creating and deploying software is a key part of your job. With these tools, you will be able to ensure you have what you need to keep things going.

Git, Visual Studio Online and Perforce

These are examples of source control systems, and they allow for the collaboration of different teams on a specific project. These tools also make it easier for the organization to manage any updates and changes.

Nagios, Munin, Sensu

It is imperative that as a DevOps professional, you track and measure performance. You have to understand the principles and philosophy behind the many tools available at your disposal to help you implement the tool effectively.

Big picture thinking

Many DevOps engineers may be excellent software engineers, but sometimes, they cannot envision the larger picture and identify what makes sense to the client. As DevOps synergizes the needs and wants of multidisciplinary teams and applications, a successful DevOps engineer cannot lose sight of the big picture. This helps avoid the creation of contention points and constraints between projects.

Network awareness

A DevOps engineer should always be aware of the network.

Testing

Strong testing skills are essential to be a successful DevOps engineer, as automation is based on testing.

Soft Skills

DevOps engineers bring together different teams to work towards achieving a common goal. Working with people is key, and therefore, a successful DO engineer must possess strong communication and interpersonal skills. A great DevOps engineer is always curious to constantly learn new things, persistently generate questions and listen to answers to brainstorm for new ideas and welcome new challenges.

Security training

DevOps professionals do not need to be expert security professionals, but they will benefit tremendously from being trained in software security. This is because, at faster cycles, vulnerabilities in code can be introduced just as quickly. Therefore, DevOps engineers must be able to write secure code to safeguard applications against attack, as well as defend them against common cybersecurity vulnerabilities.

Customer-first mindset

A DevOps engineer does not necessarily have to maintain contact with external clients, but they will face different types of end users or customers. To ensure that the team maintains a strong relationship with the client, it is important to prioritize, empathize and be transparent regardless of the number of requests that come from the operations, development and product teams. A great DevOps engineer is always concerned about delivering a product with high quality and value to the customer. They also want to measure and understand how the end user perceives their work. By doing this, they develop the right instincts and know how to optimize the process to achieve success.

Collaboration

An organization that wants to implement DevOps must always put the team and the customer ahead of an individual in the team, and therefore strong DevOps professionals must be excellent team members and help widen bottlenecks by assisting co-workers when necessary. A DevOps engineer should also learn to multitask. DevOps engineers get requests from numerous clients at the same time and find themselves putting out fires at the same time. So, the ability to work on multiple tasks at the same time is crucial.

Chapter Six
| Different Types of Deployment |

The four important types of deployment are:

Minimum In-Service deployment

In this type, the number of instances that stay in-service when you are building the application is mentioned. Therefore, this allows you to deploy as many targets as possible. This step is repeated until every server in the network has been updated.

Rolling application updates

Consider these as an extension of minimum in-service deployments. Instead of defining the number of containers that should remain online, we specify the maximum number of containers that need to be updated in parallel.

Blue/Green deployment

When following this method, an infrastructure is replicated for a short period. This replicated infrastructure now hosts the new application, while the old infrastructure continues running until testing completes and the new stack is incorporated. This was an expensive deployment method but not anymore, thanks to the Cloud. Once testing is finished, the application is switched over to the new version and the old stack is closed.

A/B testing

A/B deployments are similar to Blue/Green ones, except that a small amount of traffic is transferred to the new green environment. Switching environments in this method are more straightforward and precise way than Blue/Green deployment.

Lastly, deployment cycles may also vary based on the sensitivity and impact of the final product. For example, Amazon deploys new code around every 30 minutes on its website, but Southwest Airlines only deploys its patches twice a week as strict aviation laws are imposed to ensure rigid testing of aircraft systems.

Key Work Outputs

Overall, a DevOps engineer must ensure that the delivery pipeline is trustworthy and free of delays. On a day-to-day basis, other important contributions include:

- Guiding operations and development teams if there is an issue

- Reviewing, managing and monitoring technical operations

- Developing a continuous build environment to improve the speed of the development and deployment software

- Managing teams

Chapter Seven
|DevOps Engineer versus Other Engineers|

Difference between DevOps Engineer and Build and Release Engineer

DevOps Engineers and Build and Release Engineers have very similar roles, as they both need to identify ways to develop and deploy software. This chapter provides further information on what their responsibilities are and how different the roles are from one another.

Responsibilities of DevOps Engineers vs. Build and Release Engineers

Build and Release engineers and DevOps engineers must understand the technical requirements of a business or a project if they want to make it easier for them to build software. Some companies interchange these titles or bring a professional from each discipline onto the team. A DevOps engineer will create a pipeline that will be used to deliver stacks and tools to the development team. A build and release engineer will use various automation tools like Version One, Ansible or Jenkins to improve the process of building, testing and releasing the program to the end users.

DevOps Engineers

A DevOps engineer will work on Agile development teams and with other foundation architects and developers. They will design the build for the application and will suggest some simple, cost-effective methods to begin the process. These engineers work towards creating an automated development practice that will allow the team to develop the product faster and release it to the end user for feedback. Additionally, a DevOps engineer also improves the process of delivering the software to the end user. They do this by constantly updating the software since they will test every prototype during the development and delivery stages of the process. This will allow them to identify any operations issues and fix them. Some responsibilities include:

- Creating a style guide for applications and software.

- Maintaining the goals of the company to improve the performance of the product.

- Tracking any bottleneck issues using different deployment programs and updates.

- Understanding different tools like Puppet, Chef, and Bamboo.

Build and Release Engineers

A Build and Release Engineer will create and maintain the infrastructure which is called the source control system or the build system. This system is full of tools that will make it easier to build the software and deploy it to the end user.

83

They will need to design the scripts and tools that the developers will use to build the software. These scripts can either be written in Java or Python. A part of their job is to identify a way to seamlessly integrate the many software updates by using continuous delivery pipelines. These pipelines will take the updates to the end user in a faster way. Some responsibilities include:

- Using Unix or Linux operating systems during the build process.

- Reviewing the code that is used for the build architecture.

- Creating add-ins or plugins that will improve the process.

- Looking for solutions to avoid automation issues and integrating those solutions into the system.

DevOps versus Site Reliability Engineering

There is a lot of confusion between the

two titles, and this confusion has led to a debate about what these engineers do. In fact, many people believe that these roles are the same. There is a lot in common with these roles, especially when you consider the underlying objectives – automating, bridging the gap between the development and operations team, and scaling. However, there, is a significant difference between the two.

A dynamic organization that wants to scale at an aggressive pace will always want to lay the foundation or base for an IT department which can be both agile and nimble. For this, they will need to request the engineering department to create a foundation that can support their goals. The leads of these teams will need to use automation tools to ensure that the infrastructure is widely available for multiple teams. There are two disciplines that one must consider in this instance – site reliability engineering (SRE), which is where an architect develops a fully automated infrastructure for IT, and DevOps, a combination of the Agile and Lean processes, which allows the developers to view the infrastructure as a piece of code.

Most often, IT infrastructure is built or constructed in small parts or segments as the company grows. The systems are all configured to ensure that they serve the day-to-day needs of the business. Also, the business will make changes to the infrastructure whenever necessary. A system administrator plays a major role in ensuring that the infrastructure is maintained regularly and system updates are always made to protect the infrastructure and maintain a productive environment. The administrators will spend hours, and sometimes days to ensure that everything is working correctly.

Sophisticated IT departments will use automated scripts right from the start to reduce the dependency of the infrastructure on the administration. The system architect or engineer can then include patches, management, and policy over the network using a centralized management system. This system can then be used to monitor the environment and detect any potential issues in the infrastructure before it causes any hindrance to the process.

An SRE is always focused on the role of a system engineer to maintain the infrastructure. This role applies to the production environment. DevOps is a practice that a business can use to automate or simplify a development team and reduce or remove their non-production environments.

There is a significant difference regarding the type of environment you are in and the focus on coding between DevOps and SRE. A DevOps engineer will always stick to the side of testing and creation since these departments are dynamic. These departments also embrace the Agile and Lean methods to help their teams run. This means that the processes must be automated.

A developer will leverage different automation tools like Chef or Puppet to assist or support the teams with this challenge. DevOps and SRE share common ground since the development engineer is always at the top of the pyramid. They will architect a culture and a system that will allow the organization to automate the delivery of tasks or infrastructure within the process.

In other words, new roles are being developed, namely the SRE and DevOps engineers, to help the IT industry run efficiently. As the industry begins to grow, these practices will continue to evolve and newer practices will be developed. You must remember that it is operational efficiency that drives change. These forms of efficiency support the process of innovation and allow the IT department as a whole to run more fluidly.

Cloud Engineer versus DevOps Engineer

Both DevOps Engineers and Cloud Engineers use different computer languages like CSS and Java. The latter use these languages to design remote platforms where the data and files can be stored and accessed. The former creates the Agile team, which helps to facilitate the successful deployment of products and services by splitting the time that the developers spend on designing the software and deploying it to the customers. DevOps engineers can also assist with the development of cloud computing platforms, and they can work with downloadable software and online applications. Cloud engineers only design cloud-computing platforms for numerous companies. DevOps engineers, on the other hand, focus on improving the development and release cycle of software development by using the resources in the company effectively.

Cloud Engineers

A cloud engineer can create a remote network that a company can use to store, share and communicate data. Companies can also perform big data analysis, test and develop applications, and store back-ups of their data. Since the cloud architecture is massive, it can suit multiple users, and the cloud platform can handle large volumes of data. To become a cloud engineer, you must first understand the company's business plan and work towards creating a system that will fit their needs. If you want to learn more about the company, you should speak to the staff. This will help you determine the requirements, including what platform you want to use and why. As a cloud engineer, this will help you create a roadmap. You can then execute the design by developing a cloud infrastructure system. The job responsibilities include:

- Identifying creative cloud solutions

- Ensuring that the platform is compatible with Linux, iOS and Windows systems.

- Protecting the information stored over the cloud.

- Developing and monitoring the

cloud.

- Updating drivers and firmware as needed.

DevOps Engineers

A DevOps engineer collaborates with the operations and development team to develop a rapid release and reliable pipeline for various software and updates. This involves the development of custom automation tools, the improvement of operations and the standardization of technology. As an Agile team member, the goal of the engineer should be to increase the speed of the processes that are involved in the creation and development of software. This will cover extensive technical responsibilities including automating the process for developers and tracking bugs or errors in the design. The engineer can also choose to document the procedures being used to build and maintain the deployment and configuration frameworks and create a guide regarding the best standards and practices. Some responsibilities include:

- Identifying new sections in the process to automate.

- Utilizing automated configuration tools like Puppet and Chef.

- Deploying and maintaining web-based applications.

- Monitoring different security issues.

- Measuring the performance of the team against any business outcomes.

Systems Engineer versus DevOps Engineer

Both systems engineers and DevOps engineers work only on office settings and primarily focus on technological advances. These engineers also attempt to bring different teams and departments together. DevOps engineers identify ways to connect the software development teams and deployment teams, while Systems engineers allow employees from different departments to share information and maintain transparency, thereby allowing them to work efficiently.

DevOps Engineers

A DevOps engineer works closely with software teams and uses different programming languages like Python and Java to create a cloud system or any other web-based application, like Netflix. These applications are already available to the user. The objective of a DevOps engineer is to develop software that will automatically update itself, which means that the user does not have to worry about updating the software. The engineer will need to identify a way to update the software remotely by using pipelines that will take the new code to the customer. It is always a good idea to create a product that is made up of smaller modules or units. This will make it easier for the engineer to automate the process. Some key responsibilities include:

- Placing all the changes in the code in a single system, which will then be tested.

- Understanding how the software can grow when users save some information on it.

- Tracking the feedback loop and ensuring that feedback is taken into account before building the next user story or feature.

- Designing an environment for a new user, which is intuitive and automatic.

Systems Engineers

A Systems Engineer will design computer systems that bring software, hardware, and employees together. They will first consider the current system that is followed in the company, and identify the gaps in the system using data modelling. This method allows them to view the workflow. They will then work with the executives in the company and develop a contract that will outline the amendments that the new system should make and how it should improve the old system. This contract will also list the functions of the system. A system engineer will use this to estimate the cost of a project and develop visuals that the programmer can use. System Engineers also monitor the productivity and the reports from the new system to make modifications. The job responsibilities include:

- Gathering all the necessary input about the system by interviewing customers or end users.

- Suggesting or looking at alternative system elements to minimize cost.

- Building and developing prototypes.

- Supervising the integration to ensure that every part of the system works together.

Tools Engineer versus DevOps Engineer

A tool is a specialized software application that is designed to facilitate the work of artists, programmers, and

95

designers. These tools are often found in the game development world. It is the tool engineer's responsibility to create and maintain software for the game studio. A game development studio uses many third-party systems like Houdini, Maya, and Unreal engines to bring environments and characters to life. Some studios still rely on in-house engineers to maintain and develop systems that are designed to meet the needs of a specific game.

Duties

A tools engineer is a professional who is hired to develop the foundation of a new software system. They will be involved in the design of the system during the initial stages of building the software. When a proprietary application is in place, the engineer is then brought on board. They are now responsible for helping the system adapt to the changing needs of the environment or the game studio by contributing new programs or codes. They must also identify ways to evolve the software, regardless of whether it is a porting pipeline 3-D art suite or a game engine.

A Tools Engineer is tasked with teaching every other programmer the fine points of the system. They should also work closely with character riggers, animators and other developers to fully understand the capabilities of the application. When a member of the designing staff insists on implementing new features in the game, the engineer must make those changes quickly and ensure that there are positive results. A similar position also exists in software companies in the animation, visual effects and game industries. The objective is to create a robust and functional software tool that will allow programmers, designers, and animators to work faster. This will ensure that the game reaches the hands of the customers quickly.

Skills & Education

It is always recommended that a Tools Engineer have a formal education in game design, software engineering or computer programming. They should also have a college degree in some related field, such as a certification in advanced mathematics.

A Tools Engineer should also know how to code in the C++ languages, and any other languages based on the game development studio. Employers always hire engineers or programmers who can write a program or code that is adaptable and portable. Your code should communicate with your fellow team members in the same way that you communicate with your superiors. It is also a good idea to obtain a certification in game art or 3-D graphics.

Related Careers

If you want to become a DevOps engineer, you can also look at some other related careers like Scrum Product Owner. Both these professionals must be familiar with the requirements of the software. Regardless of what field you choose to enter, you can switch to other related careers if you do not enjoy your work.

Chapter Eight
|Micro-Service and DevOps Engineers|

Micro-Service Engineer

Microservices are services that can be deployed separately. These services perform specific business functions and only communicate over a web interface. A microservice is used to develop an application. A DevOps team will include smaller pieces of functionality in a microservice, and combine multiple microservices to buildlarge infrastructure. Therefore, you can view a microservice as a building block. There are many advantages that a microservice provides over monolith-type architecture. Microservices can remove SPOFs or single points of failure. They do this by ensuring that issues in one service do not affect any ofher service in the infrastructure. You can scale individual microservices to increase capacity. DevOps teams can improve or extend functionality by including new microservices that do not affect other parts of the application. Also, using microservices can boost team velocity.

DevOps Architect

DevOps Architects paint a bigger picture of the application and provide a foundation to build the product. They function in a manner analogous to an architect designing a house, in that they develop blueprints for an application, enabling a predictive framework to be formed. Overall, they bring in comprehensive practices that can establish a suitable DevOps channel across the entire organization.

DevOps in Banking

DevOps plays a big role in banking. An increasing number of banks are now shifting from on-premise server-based systems to cloud-based systems such as AWS, and therefore there is a constant requirement to hire DevOps engineers in this sector. Successful implementation of all DevOps targets is necessary because online banking portals are highly sensitive, meaning they need to be reliable, safe and secure. With customers trying to access their accounts and funds online, instant deployment is critical to avoid infiltration and exploitation of loopholes. For this reason, a DevOps engineer working with a banking institution must be able to work with cloud-based services and ensure smooth and safe product deployment.

AWS Certified DevOps Engineer

AWS certified engineers are validated for their technical expertise in provisioning, operating and managing distributed application systems on the AWS platform. The concepts or techniques that one needs to master to obtain this certification are the following:

- Implementation and management of continuous delivery systems on the AWS platform

- Understanding and automating security controls and compliance validation

- Defining and deploying monitoring, metrics and logging systems on the AWS platform

- Implementing high availability, scalable systems

- Designing, managing and maintaining tools to automate operational processes

As AWS is now becoming the industry standard for DevOps practices, and DevOps engineers certified by AWS are highly sought after by other organizations looking to fill their DevOps positions.

Chapter Nine
| DevOps Tools |

This chapter lists some of the tools that a DevOps Engineer must be aware of.

Nagios and Icinga

Nagios is a tool that enables teams to monitor their infrastructure. There are many tools that one can use for this purpose, including Zabbix. Although many new tools have entered the industry, Nagios is highly effective since many members of the community create plugins for the tool. These plugins help DevOps engineers add new services or instances to Nagios which are not already present in the tool. Fortunately, this is not hard, and this tool can still be used to monitor infrastructure.

Icinga is an offshoot of Nagios. The creators of Icinga wanted to take Nagios to the next level with more modern features. This was done to enhance the experience of the modern user. There is still a debate in the community about which tool is better, but most companies and teams use Nagios since they are satisfied with its performance. There is a good chance that teams and organizations switch to Icinga in the future.

Monit

The simple watchdog tool Monit proves that simple tools are sometimes the most useful. The role of this tool is to ensure that any process on a machine is up and running without any errors. For instance, if there is a failure that occurs in Apache or Adobe, Monit will restart the process and make it work well with the software. One can set up Monit very easily and configure the settings to improve its efficiency. This tool is useful if you have a multi-service architecture and cater to various micro-services. If you use Monit, you must ensure that you monitor the restarts that it executes. This will help you identify problems and look for solutions instead of ignoring the failure. This can be done by monitoring the log files in the tool and ensuring that the tool alerts you whenever it restarts a process.

Elasticsearch, Logstash, Kibana or ELK

The ELK stack is one of the most common log analytics solutions developed in the modern IT industry. This tool collects logs from different services, applications, tools, servers, networks and more, and stores it in an environment. This environment then moves that information into a single location, which can be accessed by a DevOps professional to analyze. You can use this information to troubleshoot problems, reduce the time taken to solve problems and monitor services. You can also use this tool for auditing and security, which means that you can change settings and monitor the changes made in security groups. You can act on any of these activities when you receive an alert on the issue. Some companies use ELK for business intelligence and use it to monitor the users and their behaviour. You can either purchase ELK as a service or set it up on your system.

Consul.io

A consul is a great tool that you can use to discover services and configure applications that are built from several micro-services. This is an open-source tool that uses the latest technology to provide internal DNS names for a variety of services. It acts as a broker and helps you sign and register different names thereby allowing you to access servers instead of machines. Let's assume that you have a cluster of machines. You can use Consul to register these machines as one unit and access that cluster with ease. There is a lot more than you can do with this tool, and you can experiment with it to make it work better.

Jenkins

Regardless of whether you are aspiring to be a DevOps Engineer or are still a developer, you have definitely heard about Jenkins. This is not the fanciest or fastest tool, but it is easy to use it since it has a great ecosystem of add-ons and plugins. This tool is built in a way that makes it easy for a user to customize it to their purpose. You can customize the tool to create and code Docker containers, run numerous tests and improve the production or staging process. This tool is great to use, but there are some issues regarding the performance and scaling of the tool, which is not unusual. You can also explore CircleCI and Travis, which are tools that require little or no maintenance.

Docker

There are many articles available on the internet that talk about how Docker has transformed the IT environment. The tool is life changing and great, but people sometimes experience challenges with it. Most businesses use Docket in their production services, as it eases control issues and configuration management and also allows scaling by moving containers from one place to another.

Some businesses have developed a SaaS solution using a twelve-layer data processing pipeline. When you use Docker and Jenkins together, you can run the full pipeline across several, if not all layers, on a single system. There are some complications with using Docker since it takes time to build even the smallest container. As a DevOps engineer, you will also want to ensure that your developers can work rapidly and are satisfied. This can be a challenge since it is difficult to manage storage, networking, and security for a container.

Experts believe that there will be further updates made to the tool, and they welcome new management solutions using the updated version of the tool.

Ansible

Once again, simplicity is key. Ansible, like Puppet and Chef, is a configuration management tool. Experts find that Puppet and Chef are more complex to use, and suggest that one learn how to use Ansible. Puppet and Chef have a wider range of features, but it would be best to start with Ansible since it is the easiest configuration tool to learn. There are trade-offs to using Ansible where you can kill an application and build a new one using Docker containers. Through Docker, you can spin new machines, which reduces the need to upgrade the machine to different cloud instances. Ansible is often used to configure the deployment process. This tool is used to push and re-configure newly deployed machines, and the ecosystem allows users to write custom applications.

Collectd and Collectl

Collectd and Collectl are little tools that derive and store statistics about the systems on which they run. When compared to other tools, they are flexible. Using them, a user can measure a variety of system metrics. These tools are unlike other logs in the sense that they can measure multiple parameters in parallel. Some systems use these tools to measure performance parameters, and these values are then shipped to the ELK-as-a-service platform. Some organizations wrap a Collectd or Collectl agent in a container and then push it to all the servers using Ansible. The agent will collect information every few minutes or seconds and ship that information to the ELK. This will allow the business to send alerts and run reports whenever necessary.

Git (GitHub)

The Linux Community needed a Source Control Management (SCM) software through which one could support distributed systems, and this is why GitHub was created. GitHub is the most common source management tool, and it is used by many companies. It was run internally for a short period before the developers realized that they could make it a hub. GitHub has amazing features like pull requests and forking. Apart from this, GitHub can connect to

Jenkins and help with the integration of tools and the deployment of the product or service. This is a tool that most people may have heard about, but it should be a tool you know well since it adds great value to you.

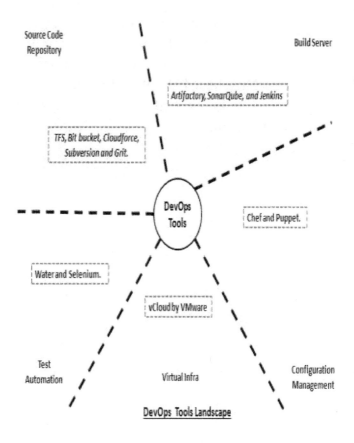

Source Code
Repository

Build Server

Artifactory, SonarQube, and Jenkins

TFS, Bit bucket, Cloudforce,
Subversion and Grit.

DevOps
Tools

Chef and Puppet.

Water and Selenium.

vCloud by VMware

Test
Automation

Virtual Infra

Configuration
Management

DevOps Tools Landscape

Chapter Ten
|The Career Path|

A DevOps practitioner is one of the highest paid IT professionals in today's market. The demand for these practitioners is increasing rapidly since many organizations have started to use DevOps practices to improve their processes. A report published by Puppetlabs: the State of DevOps stated that organizations that use the DevOps approach deploy their code at least 30 times more frequently than any other company. In addition to this, their code only fails less than fifty per cent of the time. Over the last two years, the listings for DevOps jobs on different portals like Indeed.com and LinkedIn.com have increased by fifty per cent.

DevOps Engineer Salary

The graph below was sourced from Indeed.com, and it shows that the DevOps jobs began to increase from the year 2015 onwards. Towards the end of the same year, the number of jobs available in the market went through the roof.

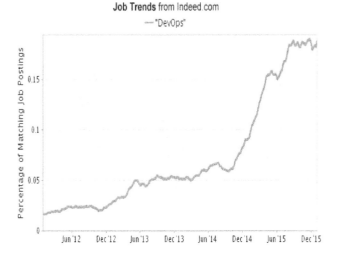

(https://www.edureka.co/blog/devops-engineer-career-path-your-guide-to-bagging-top-devops-jobs)

The salaries for DevOps jobs also increased during the year 2015, and it continues to increase today.

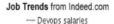

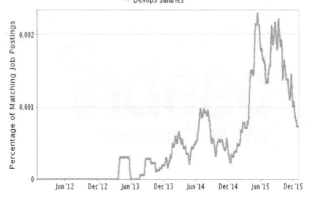

(https://www.edureka.co/blog/devops-engineer-career-path-your-guide-to-bagging-top-devops-jobs)

According to the website PayScale.com, the monthly salaries for DevOps professionals starts from $94,000, depending on experience.

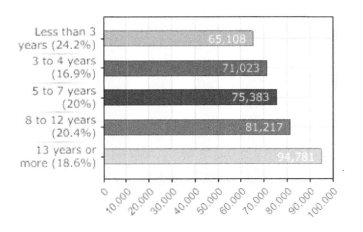

Less than 3 years (24.2%)	65,108
3 to 4 years (16.9%)	71,023
5 to 7 years (20%)	75,383
8 to 12 years (20.4%)	81,217
13 years or more (18.6%)	94,781

(https://www.edureka.co/blog/devops-engineer-career-path-your-guide-to-bagging-top-devops-jobs)

Unlike jobs in every other technological field, the DevOps field is now witnessing an impressive trend. All jobs that fall under the DevOps bracket share similar roles and opportunities. For example, if a project management role had 65,000 openings and budgeting roles had 64,000 openings, jobs around the DevOps tool (Jenkins or Chef) were higher at 69,000.

117

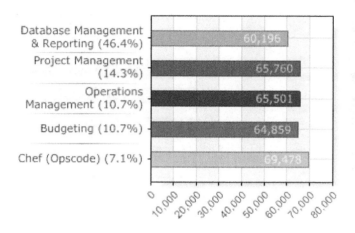

(https://www.edureka.co/blog/devops-engineer-career-path-your-guide-to-bagging-top-devops-jobs)

DevOps Roles and Responsibilities

Many new roles are now emerging around the DevOps philosophy. These include:

- DevOps Architect

- Automation Engineer

- Software Tester

- Security Engineer

118

- Integration Specialist

- Release Manager

DevOps began as an ideology or framework that different organizations could use to bring different schools of thought in an organization together. It is now a popular career path that has its own perks, and the opportunities are increasing by the day. It is truly the right time for you to start exploring the path of a DevOps engineer. You can begin your training now and take advantage of the many opportunities that are available to you.

How Do You Start?

You may have many questions. How do you prepare for an interview? How do you know where to start? How do you land a job?

The Career Credential Challenge

Unfortunately, there are very few formal training programs in DevOps, but it is easy to find a training school and obtain a certification for many IT careers. If you want to code or write programs, you should go to college and obtain a degree in Computer Science. Alternatively, you can teach yourself how to code and apply your skills to a startup or a small company that does not worry about credentials.

If you want to work on system administration, you can master in Computer Science and obtain additional certifications in Linux or Unix. You can also become a database administrator by taking up courses available on the internet. When it comes to some form of training in DevOps, there are not many colleges or schools that offer training and certification.

No institution offers higher learning in DevOps or even courses in it. There are only a handful of certificate programs and tests that are available on the internet, but these are from organizations that do not have any DevOps career opportunities.

Alternatively, you can become a certified DevOps professional for platforms like

Amazon Web Services, but cannot become a DevOps professional as a whole.

Start Developing Skills

In the earlier chapters, we covered some of the important skills that a DevOps professional should have, so you should focus on how to develop those skills.

College Courses

It is always a good idea to start with a degree in Electrical Engineering, Computer Science, or a similar field. It may not provide all the information that you need to begin as a DevOps engineer after graduation, but it still gives you a strong technical foundation. This is true if you choose to take a course that covers numerous areas including philosophy or history, instead of focusing only on operating systems or programming.

DevOps MOOCs

You can find many open online courses (MOOCs) on numerous websites. EdX, Udacity and Coursera offer DevOps courses. Most employers may not be impressed if you complete a MOOC since a college degree will take precedence over that certificate, but it can still help you stand out. You will also get training in DevOps, which is oriented towards real-world applications instead of focusing only on theory like in college.

Public Demonstration of Skills

If you have written a tool that will solve a software management task, you should ensure that you publish it on GitHub. If you have thoughts on how to coordinate software delivery across different systems, you should write a blog and share that information. You should always be ready to demonstrate your achievements and skills.

The article you write or the code you develop does not necessarily have to go viral for you to advance in your work. When you make your work publicly available, you can use it as a passive indicator of your expertise and also show the industry that you are committed to contributing to the community. This is always a good thing.

Following the DevOps Conversation

You have to ensure that you are always up to date with the conversation taking place in the industry. People no longer talk about DevOps the way that they used to. This process not only involves the IT operations team or the development team but also includes the security engineers, quality assurance team and more. You should always strive to learn more about DevOps. It is harder to start a DevOps career than it is to land a technical job, but you can do it if you find the right educational resources and use those resources in the right way. Ensure that you immerse and involve yourself in the DevOps community.

Chapter Eleven
| How to market yourself as a DevOps Engineer |

In today's world, the DevOps career path is a satisfying career option and one of the most profitable options in the IT industry. According to a survey conducted by Incapsula, the median of salaries for DevOps careers is between $104,000 and $129,230. The salary is dependent on the size of the team. When you compare the salaries on Payscale.com, you will see that there is a stark difference between the salaries of DevOps professionals and non-DevOps IT professionals.

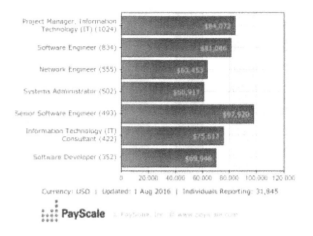

Currency: USD | Updated: 1 Aug 2016 | Individuals Reporting: 31,945

PayScale

(https://techbeacon.com/5-ways-make-yourself-marketable-devops-engineer)

How to Become an Indispensable DevOps Engineer

As mentioned in the earlier chapter, it is important to build your profile to land a DevOps job. So, what should you do to build on the skill sets and the experience that you need? How do you get your personal brand out into the market to land a job? This chapter lists some of the best ways to make yourself an indispensable DevOps engineer. This input is based on sayings by experts in the field.

125

Start Cross-training now

Regardless of whether you are an operations manager or a developer, it is never too late to acquire skills that are outside your current role and comfort zone. This is only if you want to become a DevOps professional. A developer has an edge over the Operations professional since they have experience in coding and programming. Also, they understand the needs of a developer. It is always great if a DevOps professional was previously a developer rather than just an IT professional.

A DevOps engineer with a developer background will have more in-depth knowledge and understanding of the tools that the developers use. Therefore, they can leverage that knowledge to improve processes. The key is to always look for a different way to apply a concept from a previous role to a new position.

You have to use your experience and skills as a software engineer or developer to build tools, and you should

126

not focus only on the development of software. For some examples, you can look at the many open-source projects that Netflix has written. If you want to become a DevOps Engineer, you should try to work on operational tasks. If the team does not work on any such tasks, you should sit with the operations team and see what work they do during deployments.

Some managers refer hiring developers as DevOps engineers; however, some managers will still consider you for the position of a DevOps engineer if you have experience as a system administrator. All you need to do is work on your scripting and programming skills. In the past, many system administrators were called upon to automate tasks like configuration, provisioning, and employment since it was difficult for them to develop scripting skills. This means that they must always put in the time to gain experience on Puppet or Chef scripting, develop a familiarity with Shell and Linux environments and gain some knowledge and experience in programming languages. They can learn languages like Python, Perl, Ruby, and Bash.

You should always document your work in the form of code and spend sufficient time understanding automation frameworks that will help you automate deployments and provisioning.

Build Skills in the Job You Have For the Job You Want

Many companies offer the position of a plum DevOps engineer, and they only select applicants who have already worked with DevOps. An IT professional who does not have a DevOps title will find it easier to land these roles if they can include DevOps-minded tasks and responsibilities to their existing roles. They should do this regardless of whether they change their job title or not. Take John Behling as an example – Field Nation who was recently hired as the Senior DevOps engineer for Field Nation. Before this, he worked as a

System Administrator since 2008.

John mentioned that he always spent some time to automate tasks to make his life easier. He also mentioned that things began to change in the year 2014 when he began the role of a System Administrator. In this role, he was expected to develop a server that several development teams could use. It was then that he began to call himself a DevOps Engineer, as he was being used to complete tasks for the new-school system administration work.

Automate Processes

Rick Tai, Head of Engineering at Reflective, mentioned that he always hires people who can complete cumbersome processes within a few minutes or hours. This means that he will only hire a DevOps engineer who can use automation tools to manage deployments and servers. Behling agreed that it is important for an aspiring DevOps engineer to master different automation practices and tools, as this will improve their marketability and increase their salary. Behling says that one should always study automation, and believes that one should never be stuck with tedious manual work since they will not be happy about where they are. If you want to automate tasks, you should have a deep understanding of the task. So, when you spend time on automation, you will gain new insights into the technology that you are supporting.

Involve Yourself with the Community

As mentioned in the previous chapter, you should always involve yourself with the DevOps community, as you can only market yourself if you build on your skills and identify a way to display those skills. You can only do this if you are involved with the DevOps community. There is not just one way to go about this since a process depends on every individual team member's skills and interests. You can either speak at industry events or write blogs or articles. Alternatively, you can stay in touch with your colleagues through different online platforms. Behling says that you should also try to work on an open-source project since that will have a larger impact on the community.

When you work on an open-source project that is related to DevOps, you will be giving yourself a big opportunity since you can show the world what you know and what you can do with your skills. Presenting at meetups and talking in small gatherings is important. Also, you can participate in public Slack channels and answer questions. This will help you improve your brand and visibility.

Eric Sigler, Director of Site Reliability at PagerDuty believes that DevOps engineers do not always have to be involved in the community. He believes that people who do not see community involvement as mandatory gain more from it. He believes that one should not approach the community only to develop a career. People should always use the community to connect with other professionals and gain exposure to new ideas. Since every person in the community brings their enthusiasm, they can provide a unique support system.

Demonstrate Empathy and Curiosity

Sigler believes that empathy and curiosity are two soft-skill traits that a DevOps Engineer should demonstrate. If a person can demonstrate these qualities, an organization will trust that the person will care deeply about the company, their role in the company and the DevOps processes.

It is easier to demonstrate curiosity since you can always develop or build a wide skill set, and also learn how to ask the right questions when you are working on a project. This will help you change for the better. It is a little difficult to show empathy since this means that you need to identify a way to build muscle memory in the ear, as listening is a big part of developing empathy. Another way to develop empathy is to put yourself in situations where you will need to communicate with others. It is crucial to translate what you do to your peers – presenting, explaining and teaching. This is because you may find a way to improve the process or logic while talking to someone else about it. You must ensure that what you are doing is not something that only you understand and that whatever you do is accessible to every member of the team.

Chapter Twelve
| Interview Questions |

This chapter lists some questions that you may be asked in an interview.

<u>Question</u>: **Explain or define DevOps.**

<u>Answer</u>: You should ensure that you cover some or all of the points mentioned below:

- DevOps improves the collaboration and communication between the operations and business development teams. Through DevOps, you can unify different teams within an organization.

- DevOps is not just about the tools. It is mainly about involving different people and the process.

- The Lean and Agile processes inspire DevOps

- Through DevOps, you can automate the development, operation and release processes.

- Through DevOps, you can increase the speed of delivering applications to end-users.

- DevOps focuses on the improvement of processes through continuous feedback loops.

<u>Question</u>: **What are some prerequisites that are necessary for DevOps Implementation?**

<u>Answer</u>: The prerequisites include:

- The need for change must be communicated across the organization

- The senior management should commit to the values of DevOps

- Versions of the deployed software

- Automated testing

135

- Automated tools to maintain compliance

- Automated deployment

Question: **What are the best practices of DevOps implementation?**

Answer: The implementation of DevOps will vary for different organizations. In today's market, organizations and businesses want to deliver their products faster. This answer focuses on how you can use DevOps to improve communication between the organization, including the operations team, and the customers.

- The DevOps implementation should always align with business goals. This means that the organization must agree that there is a need for change.

- The implementation should encourage collaboration and communication between the operations and development teams.

- It is important to automate processes, and during the SDLC stages, one should automate processes whenever possible. This will facilitate the implementation of DevOps.

- Tools that are used in DevOps should integrate and work well together. You should always look for tools that come from one vendor or look at open source tools that integrate with your organization's values.

- You should always include the CI and CD practices or tools in your implementation. Therefore, you should identify ways to continuously integrate code with testing, and continuously deliver the product to customers.

- The operations team must ensure that the applications work well at all levels. They may need to work with the development team if necessary to build or construct tools that will help to build or incorporate the right monitoring methods into various applications.

- Encourage feedback from your customers to ensure that there is continuous improvement. This will ensure that the process improves continuously and that the quality of the software improves.

Question: **What are the components of DevOps?**

Answer: The following are the components of DevOps:

- Continuous monitoring

- Continuous integration

- Continuous delivery

- Continuous testing

Question: **Define Continuous Integration.**

Answer: Continuous integration is an important part of the Agile process. A developer will work on a user story or a feature during a sprint and make changes to the developed version continuously. When the code is committed, the work of the developers is integrated with the final product. The team will then perform the build regularly based on a schedule or check-in. Therefore; continuous integration is a practice that forces developers to integrate the changes they make to the product with other changes to obtain feedback from customers.

Question: Define **Continuous Delivery.**

Answer: Continuous delivery ensures that the features that the developers build reach the customers very quickly. This is an extension of continuous integration. It is during this process that the changes go through testing and quality assurance tests. When there are no further changes to make, the product is moved to the production system

139

where it will be deployed.

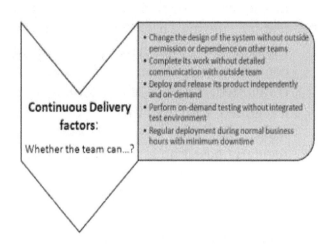

Continuous Delivery factors:

Whether the team can...?

- Change the design of the system without outside permission or dependence on other teams
- Complete its work without detailed communication with outside team
- Deploy and release its product independently and on-demand
- Perform on-demand testing without integrated test environment
- Regular deployment during normal business hours with minimum downtime

Question: **Define Continuous Testing.**

Answer: As mentioned earlier, teams do their best to make changes to their products and deliver them to their customers very quickly. This can only happen when the product goes through sufficient automation and unit tests. Therefore, the team should identify ways to validate the code or script and ensure that the code is in line with the vision.

Question: **Define Continuous Monitoring.**

Answer: When the application is fully developed and deployed, the team must monitor how it performs in the market. It is important to monitor the products since it will help the team identify defects at an early stage.

Question: **How should you approach a project if you need to implement DevOps?**

Answer: You can use the following approach to implement DevOps for a project, but this approach will vary depending on the organization or the project.

- Stage 1: Before you implement DevOps, you should assess the existing process and see how it is implemented for at least three weeks. You can use at least five applications to see how the process works, identify any improvements and also develop a roadmap that you can use for the implementation of DevOps. This assessment should be performed by a senior DevOps architect.

- Stage 2: You can then perform a pilot POC that you can use to show the end-to-end working of the DevOps implementation. When the customers accept this implementation, you can begin the actual implementation of DevOps. You should also hand the project over and roll out a plan for the various projects involved. You can also include training sessions whenever necessary to understand the various tools and the process.

- Stage 3: You should now implement the DevOps model, and run all processes through that implementation. This means that you should follow the values of DevOps.

Question: **Can one apply the DevOps process to a traditional process or waterfall process? What is the**

significance of the Agile movement in DevOps implementation?

Answer: In the waterfall process, the first step is to gather requirements. Once they are gathered, the team will develop or design the system, implement it, and test it. The final step is to deploy the final product to the customers or end users. The problem with this process is that there is a significant gap between the building and deployment of the developed product, which makes it very hard to get feedback from the end users.

The solution to this is to use Agile processes to improve the functions of the operations and development team. You must abide by the principles of the Agile process to ensure that the DevOps implementation works. This is because DevOps is an offshoot of the Agile process.

DevOps is focused on releasing the software promptly, which allows the team to obtain feedback quickly.

Question: **State the difference between continuous delivery and continuous deployment**.

Answer: If you look at an Agile sprint, there are many user stories or features that the team will develop, test and deploy to the end user. Based on the priorities and needs of customers, not all user stories or features are deployed. Therefore, in continuous delivery, it is important to ensure that the code is always ready to be deployed.

When it comes to continuous deployment, the changes developed go through various stages of testing before the user story or feature moves to the production environment.

Question: How much experience do you have working on DevOps projects?

Answer: You should explain to the interviewer what your tasks were and what your role was as a DevOps Engineer. You should also explain what type of environment you worked in, and the projects that you worked on. If you have an automated process before, you should also provide information about it and talk about how you supported other teams. This will show the interviewer that you took up enough responsibility and also identified ways to automate processes in the organization. You should also talk about some of the Agile processes and tools that you may have used in end-to-end automation. If you have experience working with cloud computing platforms like AWS, you should let the interviewer know about that too.

Question: **What are the most important DevOps tools that are used in the industry?**

Answer: You can list the following tools:

- Jira

- Bamboo

- GIT/SVN

- Artifactory/Nexus

- Jenkins

- Bitbucket

- Docker

- SonarQube

- IBM Urbancode Deploy / CA-RA

- Chef / Puppet /Ansible

- Nagios / Splunk

<u>Question</u>: **Explain the uses of some or all the tools that you have mentioned above, and how you can use them in the DevOps model.**

<u>Answer</u>: If you know how or why the different tools are used, you should let the interviewer know immediately.

- **Jira**: This tool is used for issue management and project planning.

- **GitHub**: This tool is used for continuous integration and version control

- **Jenkins**: This is an open source tool that is used for continuous integration. It can also be used in continuous delivery.

- **SonarQube**: This tool is used to analyze the code.

- **JFrog Artifactory**: This tool is used as a binary repository manager.

- **Chef/Ansible/Puppet**: These tools are used for continuous delivery, application deployment, and configuration management.

- **IBM Urbancode Deploy/ CA RA**: This tool is used for continuous delivery.

- Nagios/Spunk: This tool is used for continuous monitoring.

You can now shed some light on a sample workflow of the DevOps implementation.

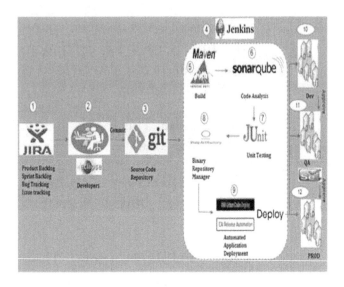

(https://www.edureka.co/blog/intervie
w-questions/top-devops-interview-
questions-2016/)

- In most agile processes, the tasks,
  defects and user stories are stored
  in JIRA. These processes are then
  assigned to developers and
  product owners.

- The developers will select the
  tasks that are assigned to them
  and work on development. The
  source code or primary version of

148

the product is stored in the Git. The developers will make necessary changes to the code in Git, and it is then shared with the other developers through GitHub.

- Jenkins is a continuous integration tool which will pull the code out on every run or check-in. This is dependent on a schedule that the team builds using tools like ANT and Maven.

- Once the J2EE WAR files are produced, they are controlled and stored in a binary repository manager like Nexus or Artifactory.

- Unit testing will use Code Analysis and Junit along with SonarQube. This process is also automated.

- When the above process is fully complete, the continuous delivery section of the process is performed. This is performed on different environments based on different tools like Deploy / CA RA or IBM UrbanCode. Continuous Testing is used in appropriate test environments.

- Continuous monitoring is an ongoing activity that takes place in the production environment.

Question: **Define configuration management in terms of infrastructure. List the popular tools used.**

Answer: Configuration management uses different practices and tools to automate delivery and infrastructure operations. This process is about maintaining the server to ensure that it is always ready to be used. The tools used in this space are Chef, Ansible and Puppet.

Question: **Which scripting tools should you use in DevOps?**

Answer: Ruby and Python

Question: **What are the roles involved in DevOps?**

Answer: We have covered this in the first few chapters of the book. There are two roles involved in DevOps:

- DevOps Architect: The person responsible for the complete DevOps process.

- DevOps Engineer: This person should know Agile, Lean, SCM, CI/CD and should know how to set up automation tools. He should also possess database management and infrastructure automation skills. A person who has skills in coding and programming, and knows how to deploy projects or work as a system administrator can become a DevOps engineer.

Question: **Have you ever used the cloud to develop or implement DevOps? If yes, which platform or software have you used?**

Answer: You should familiarize yourself with the following computing platforms:

- Microsoft Azure

- Amazon Web Services (AWS)

- Google Cloud

Question: **List some of the metrics that aided in the success of DevOps.**

Answer: Some of the examples that you can mention are listed below:

- The most important factor that one should consider is the speed of delivery. This means that the developers should not take too long to complete an item and push it into the production environment.

- The next aspect to consider would be the deployment of the user story or feature, and how long it would take if the process was automated.

- It is also important to track the number of defects or bugs identified in the environment with respect to the production environment. This is extremely important since it will consider features that need to be released sooner rather than later. Since DevOps uses Agile principles, it helps to reduce defects in the production level.

- Deployments do not fail, but it is important to keep track of this. The DevOps team should identify a way to roll back or move to a previous stable version of the software.

- In a DevOps implementation, it is important to test the unit and ensure that the functional aspects of the code are tested. Depending on the changes made to the code, the DevOps team should look at what tests it will need to conduct and to what extent. It is important to ensure that the test is robust enough to withstand any changes made to the code.

- It is extremely important to identify a way to measure the average and actual time the development team takes to recover the software if there is any failure in the environment. This is defined as the mean time to recover (MTTR), and it should be very short. This means that the teams should identify a way to monitor the process.

- The performance of the application is a key metric that must be monitored, especially when a deployment is made.

- An important factor for the success of the DevOps tool is the number of bugs that the customers report. If there are too many bugs in the system, the customers will question the quality of the application.

Question: **What do you expect from a career as a DevOps professional or engineer?**

Answer: The answer here can vary depending on what you want to achieve as a DevOps professional, but you should cover the following points:

- Improve processes to enable the collaboration between the operations and development teams.

- To help different teams understand each other's visions.

- To be a part of the end-to-end delivery of the product.

Conclusion

Thank you for purchasing the book.

In recent times, many tools have been developed to improve different processes. DevOps is one of them, but most people consider it a managerial tactic rather than a tool. Through the implementation of DevOps, a business can ensure that the development and operations teams collaborate to build the best software products. This book covers all the information you need to understand what DevOps is and how you can use it to improve your business.

Hello!

*How was it? If you liked the book kindly leave a review! Any further suggestions: Kindly reach out at **valueadd2life@gmail.com***

Stephen Fleming

Sources

https://www.techrepublic.com/article/10-critical-skills-that-every-devops-engineer-needs-for-success/

https://study.com/articles/devops_engineer_vs_build_and_release_engineer.html

https://www.linkedin.com/pulse/devops-vs-site-reliability-engineering-sean-washington/

https://study.com/articles/cloud_engineer_vs_devops_engineer.html

https://www.quora.com/What-is-a-tools-engineer-How-is-it-different-than-a-DevOps-engineer-or-network-engineer

https://study.com/articles/devops_engineer_vs_systems_engineer.html

https://dzone.com/devops-tutorials-tools-news

https://theagileadmin.com/what-is-devops/

https://dzone.com/articles/devops-devops-principles

https://www.devopsagileskills.org/dasa-devops-principles/

https://dzone.com/articles/an-introduction-to-devops-principles

https://techbeacon.com/5-ways-make-yourself-marketable-devops-engineer

https://logz.io/blog/become-devops-engineer/

157

https://devopsagenda.techtarget.com/opinion/Looki
ng-for-a-DevOps-career-path-Heres-how-to-get-
started

https://www.edureka.co/blog/devops-engineer-
career-path-your-guide-to-bagging-top-devops-jobs

https://www.edureka.co/blog/interview-
questions/top-devops-interview-questions-2016/

https://www.softwaretestinghelp.com/devops-
interview-questions/

https://www.quora.com/How-does-a-DevOps-
engineer-use-Jenkins

**https://devops.com/9-open-source-devops-
tools-love/**

My Other Books available across the platforms in e-book, paperback and audible versions:

1. Blockchain Technology : Introduction to Blockchain Technology and its impact on Business Ecosystem

2. DevOps Handbook: Introduction to DevOps and its Impact on Business Ecosystem

3. Blockchain Technology and DevOps: Introduction and Impact on Business Ecosystem

4. **Love Yourself: 21-day plan for learning "Self-Love" to cultivate self-worth, self-belief, self-confidence & happiness**

5. Intermittent Fasting: 7 effective techniques of Intermittent Fasting

7 EFFECTIVE TECHNIQUES OF

INTERMITTENT FASTING

Stay Healthy,Lose Weight,
Slow Down Aging Process & Live Longer!

STEPHEN FLEMING

6. Love Yourself and intermittent Fasting(Mind and Body Bundle Book)

New Releases 2018

167

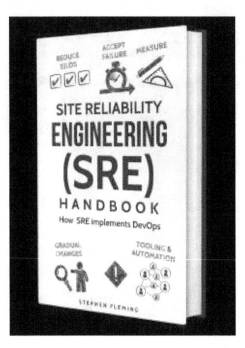

You can check all my Books on my
Amazon's Author Page

** If you prefer audible versions of these books, I have few free coupons, mail me at valueadd2life@gmail.com. If available, I would mail you the same.

Book 2:
Site Reliability
Engineering (SRE)
Handbook

How SRE Implements
DevOps

Copyright 2018 - All rights reserved.

BONUS TECHNOLOGY BOOKLET

Dear Friend,
I am privileged to have you onboard. You have shown faith in me and I would like to reciprocate it by offering the maximum value with an amazing booklet which contains the latest technology updates on DevOps and Blockchain.

"Get Instant Access to Free Booklet and Future Updates"

- Link: http://eepurl.com/dge23r

OR

- QR Code: You can download a QR code reader app on your mobile and open the link:

Preface

Well, you have been hearing a lot about DevOps lately, wait until you meet a Site Reliability Engineer!

Google is the pioneer in the SRE movement and Ben Treynor from Google defines SRE as," "what happens when a software engineer is tasked with what used to be called operations". The ongoing struggles between Development and Ops team for software releases have been sorted out by mathematical formula for green or red-light launches!

Sounds interesting, now do you know which the organizations are using SRE: Apart from Google, you can find SRE job postings from LinkedIn, Twitter, Uber, Oracle, Twitter and many more.

I also enquired about the average salary of an SRE in the USA and all the leading sites gave similar results around $130,000 per year. Also, currently the most sought job titles in the tech domain are DevOps & Site Reliability Engineer.

So do you want to know, How SRE works, what are the skill sets required, How a software engineer can transit to SRE role, How LinkedIn used SRE to smoothen the deployment process?

Here is your chance to dive into the SRE role and know what it takes to be and implement best SRE practices.

The DevOps, Continuous Delivery and SRE movements are here to stay and grow, its time you to ride the wave!

So, don't wait and take action!

1. SRE Introduction

Intro

The main function of SRE is that the system's software, hardware, and firmware will perform its tasks satisfactorily. The task being the one for which the system was designed and created. This too within a stipulated time and in a specific environment.

SRE is an engineering discipline that includes certain aspects of software engineering to tackle IT operations related issues. The main objective is the creation of ultra-scalable and extremely reliable software systems. System engineering is the parent discipline of SRE or reliability engineering. SRE emphasizes the reliability factor in product management lifecycle. Reliability or dependability is described as the capability of a system or its components to function normally in an understated condition for a stipulated period.

183

The main role of a reliability engineer is to identify and manage risks involved in assets management. These risks could adversely affect business or workshop operations. This is a broad, primary role and can be divided into three smaller and more manageable roles such as loss estimation, LCAM (Life Cycle Asset Management), and risk management.

The main difference between DevOps and SRE's is DevOps' primary focus on coding and the kind of atmosphere you are in. DevOps are at the top of the pyramid in terms of software development. They are responsible for both architecture and system culture. They deliver tasks or develop infrastructure within the development process.

The Emergence of SRE (Site Reliability Engineer)

This branch of engineering has developing importance in IT Operations. You can find more than a thousand listed on LinkedIn alone for this requirement. Although this job continues to gain importance, there is still a lot of confusion about the requirements. The SRE 2018 report has shown that the SRE role is evolving. There are many engineers who are happy in their organization but, at the same time, are struggling to explain their roles in the company. Another interesting fact highlighted in the survey was that SREs are present in all sizes of company and they hail from a range of backgrounds. It is not necessary that an ideal SRE is a generalist.

The SRE's role was first established by Google in 2003 while trying to cope up with its fast-growing production needs. Since then, several other companies have implemented SREs in their teams. Over the years the portfolio has increased with a requirement of software development and IT operational skills combined together. An SRE is expected to cover both areas of expertise.

The growth of SRE was pretty much

expected, especially in the area of complex infrastructure where constant availability and speed is of paramount significance. As Google pointed out the SRE is a single point of arbiter and responsibility between Devs and Ops teams. They ensure reliable and low latency apps delivery.

SRE is a specialized job and focuses on maintainability and reliability of large environments. SREs couple operational responsibility with the competence of software engineering to navigate system architecture. They are expected to strike the right balance between development speed and reliability by using engineering solutions to resolve operational issues.

SREs and Automation

According to a reliable survey conducted recently, the most important skill an SRE must have is automation. 92% of the SREs found automation to be the top technical skill required and 18% have indicated that their teams have automated all possible aspects of the operations process. A typical aspect of an SRE is a strong desire not to see the same issue again. This is because the issue has been automized the second time around. SRE participation in problem-solving is more dynamic as they are expected to engineer away the issues rather than just restoring the system back to normalcy. If you find that mobiles and pagers are not ringing continuously on the floor, the SREs have done their job. It means that the system is more stable and reliable, and it is time to move on to another system in the company that needs SREs.

However, you need to remember that SRE is not totally about automation. The engineers require lots of both technical and non-technical skills. The survey indicates that the SRE needs the ability to solve problems, be part of a team, work under pressure, and have strong verbal and written skills. The technical skills required include logging, monitoring, automation, infrastructure configuration, observability, scripting languages and application, and network protocols.

SREs have accepted both continuous deployment and cloud. About 65% of SREs are in the cloud and are deploying codes at least once daily. 47% deploy codes multiple times daily while 27% use it once a week. Another point to remember for the SREs is that it is a position for an experienced engineer and not for an entry-level pro. 80% of SREs have been working for more than 6 years, have a college degree, and come with IT Operations experience. Before becoming an SRE, most engineers came from system admin, development, or DevOps background.

Reporting

SREs report mainly to the engineering and operations department. However, it can be noted that SREs report more to software engineering than IT operations. This is slightly surprising as most SREs hail from an IT operations background. 25% of SREs admitted to having more than 100 such engineers under their wings. Google, for example, has 2500

SREs throughout their company. Google is looking at them to create a reliable platform and infrastructure that allows both its indigenous infrastructure and that of their GCP clientele to be stable.

SREs work in close quarters with product development software engineers. They can either be embedded with independent product development teams or separate teams working in close relations and are looking to improve maintainability and reliability. Any company that is looking to improve its software operations will benefit from building an SRE infrastructure and hiring these engineers.

If the surveys conducted are to be believed, the work culture shift can be a hindrance. Moving the job from conventional OPS to SRE can be a difficult cultural shift, not just for the engineers but also for the departments and teams involved in the change. People are still working through the transition and are still finding that the change is far more effective than before and the presence of SREs definitely provides more effective methodology than the IT OPS. Another important factor is the availability as important service indicators, notifications and alerting solutions, as they play a significant role in the tools SREs possess.

2. Principles of SRE

1. Embracing Risk

People might start expecting Google to build a 100% reliable service. The sort of platform and service that will never fail. But the fact of the matter is that increasing reliability after a certain point is not good for the service. The simple reason is that extreme reliability comes at a cost. Stability pushes the development of new features and how fast they can be delivered to users. This again increases the cost. As a result, the team will be forced to reduce the features the maker can offer. Keeping this in mind, the SRE seeks to balance the risk of feature unavailability with rapid innovation and effective operations so that the user's overall happiness with the features, service, and product performance is increased. Unreliable systems quickly lessen the confidence of the users in the system.

191

Remember, as a system is built the cost does not always increase linearly with reliability.

Service reliability management can be expensive as risk management is always costly. 100% reliability is probably not even a good target. Not only is it impossible to achieve, but it is also more dependability than users wish. Always match the service profile with the risk the business is ready to take. An error budget emphasizes the joint ownership between product development and SRE and aligns the incentives. It makes things easier in terms of release dates rate. It also diffuses tense discussions with stakeholders and allows teams to reach the same conclusion.

2. Service Level Objectives (SLOs)

It is not possible to manage a service accurately, let alone well, without knowing which behaviour matters for the service and how to evaluate these behaviours. Due to this, we are required to define and provide a certain level of service to the users whether they are using internal API or public products. We need to use experience, understanding of user requirements, and hunch when we are defining the Service Level Objectives (SLOs). The measurements thus derived describe the basic properties of matrices which are significant. Now, what values you wish the matrices to have depended on what the expected service levels are and whether you can provide the level of service. Selection of the right matrices ultimately helps in driving in the right action in case something goes wrong. It also provides the necessary confidence to the SRE team that the service is indeed good and healthy.

3. Eliminating Toil

This is one of the most important tasks to be performed by the SRE team. There is always this tendency to toil and to perform repetitive and mundane operational work providing no additional value and scaling linearly with service growth. In case all members of a team are committed to eliminating some toil every week with some quality engineering we are on the way to cleaning up the services and shift the collective efforts towards engineering for scale, development of next generation of services, and building toolchains that are cross SRE. The idea is to invent more and toil less.

4. Monitoring Distributed Systems

If you consider Google or any other empire, monitoring is an absolutely essential part of doing things right during production. In case you can't monitor a service you are at a loss and don't know what is happening. And if you are not aware of what is happening, you cannot be reliable. The SRE teams of Google are aware of the best principles and practices for building useful alerting and monitoring systems. A good alerting and monitoring system is always simple and easy to reason with.

5. Automation

Evolution of automation is a force multiplier for the SRE. However, multiplying forces does not automatically mean that the force is being applied at the right place. Doing automation mindlessly creates many problems and sometimes these problems are more than the process solves. Although it is a fact that software-based automation is better than a manual one, in most cases, it is better not to have either of the two options. A higher level system design is an autonomous system and it requires neither. In other words, the value of automation is not only in what it does but also in its wise application.

6. Release Engineering

Release engineering is not treated seriously by most companies and is an afterthought in most cases. But release engineering is critical to the overall stability of the system. Remember, most outages occur due to pushing some sort of changes or the others. It is the best way to make sure that all releases are consistent. Release engineering is a comparatively newer and faster-growing side of software engineering. It is useful in building and delivering software. Release engineers require deep knowledge of many domains, such as configuration management, development, system admin, testing, and support. Having reliable services needs you to have reliable release processes. Changes to any feature of the release procedure should be deliberate rather than unintended. SREs, take care of the process from the stage of source code to its deployment. At Google, release engineering is a particular job function.

Release engineers work with the software engineers during product development and along with SREs, they decide the steps needed for the software release. Release engineers are involved in how software is stowed in source code repository to shape rules for assembling, testing, packaging and conducting of deployment.

7. Simplicity

One of the key principles of effective software engineering is simplicity. Once this quality is lost it is very difficult to recover and recapture. The simplicity of the software is a pre-requisite to the reliability of the service. We are not being lazy when every task allotted is simplified by us. Rather we will clarify what we are trying to achieve and what is the simplest way to do it. Every time there is a "NO" from the SRE to a feature they are not restricting innovation instead, they are keeping out the cluttered distractions so that the focus remains on innovation and real engineering can move forward.

3. SRE Practices

1. Being On-Call

Constantly being on call is a duty that is critical to several engineering and operations teams in order to undertake their responsibilities. It keeps the team services available and reliable. But there are many problems with organizations having on-call rotations and responsibilities which may lead to dire consequences to the service and for the team in case it's not handled in time. Google's approach to the on-call has enabled the SREs to use engineering work as the means for scaling production responsibilities and maintaining high reliability and availability. This is despite the ever-increasing complexity of the systems and their number.

2. Emergency Response

Things break in the real world. That's life. Regardless of the size of the

198

company or the stakes involved, there is one aspect critical to the long-term health of a company. It also sets an organization apart from others. It is the emergency response and how the people involved reacting to an emergency. There are a few people who naturally respond well to an emergency. A proper response takes training and preparation. Establishment of training and testing processes needs the support of board and management in addition to staff attention. All these things are necessary for creating an environment in which teams can work towards ensuring processes, systems, and people respond correctly and promptly during an emergency.

3. Learning from Failure: The Postmortem Culture

SREs work with complex, large-scale and well-distributed systems. There is a constant enhancement with new features and the addition of new systems. Outages and incidents are pretty much inevitable given the velocity of change and the magnitude of operations. Whenever there is an incident, SREs fix the undermining issue and the services are returned to their normal operational conditions. However, unless there is a process of learning from the outages in place, they will recur many times. If they are left unchecked, they occur in a cascading effect or increase in complexity eventually overwhelming the operator and the system itself affecting end users. For these reasons, a postmortem is an essential tool for SREs. It is a well-known concept in the tech industry. It is a written record of incidents, actions taken and the impact, root causes, and follow-up actions taken to prevent the outage from happening again.

4. Handling Overload

Avoiding overload in a process is a global load balancing policy. However, no matter how well balanced your load balancing policy is, some part of the system at some stage gets overloaded. Handling the overload conditions comfortably is a basic thing in running a reliable service. One way of handling overload is by serving degraded responses. These responses are not as accurate as of the normal responses or they have less data than normal but they are easier to compute. But under extreme overload, the service cannot compute, even the degraded responses. At the point, there is no other way than having errors. However, it is critical to ensure that independent tasks are secured against the overload. Take the degraded conditions seriously. If they are ignored, many systems exhibit bad behaviour.

5. Data Processing Pipelines

The periodic pipelines in service are valuable. But if the data processing problem grows organically or is continuous, never use the periodic pipeline. Rather use the technology having characteristics similar to the Workflow. It is a fact that continuous data processing with a strong guarantee like that provided by the Workflow performs well. It also scales well on distributed cluster infrastructure and regularly produces reliable results. It is a stable and reliable system for the SRE team to maintain and manage.

6. Tracking Outages

Improving the reliability of a system is possible only if you start from a baseline and can make progress. There are devices available to track outages. Learning from past issues systematically is necessary for effective service management. Postmortems provide details on the reports of independent outages. However, they are only a part of the answer. This is because they are written for a larger impact and the smaller issues having a frequent but smaller impact and do not fall under their scope. Postmortems provide great insights for improving services but they may miss opportunities to provide similar insight in smaller individual cases. Or some other poor cost-benefit ratios. There is other information such as how many alerts did a team get during their shift, which might point to some useful information. Other similar information such as how many alerts were actionable and how many were non-actionable also provide insight into some issues. "Which services that a team is managing is producing the maximum toil?", also gives some useful information.

7. Reliable Product Launches

Internet companies such as Google can launch new products and features at great speed with rapid iterations than compared to conventional companies. The role of SRE in the process is to make the rapid change of pace possible without compromising the site stability. Google has created a dedicated team of "Launch Coordination Engineers" for the purpose. They consult with the various engineering teams regarding the technical aspects of the software launch. They create a launch checklist with common questions about the launching and try to resolve issues. The checklist has proved to be a reliable tool for ensuring dependable launches.

4. SRE Implementation

1. Context vs. Control in SRE

One of the most important things to focus on in SRE is providing context instead of utilizing processes that are working around control. But that is the way most SRE operates. So, what is context versus control in SRE? By context, it is meant providing additional and relevant information which allows an engineer to understand the rationalism behind any request. At a higher level, the context related to availability is the availability of micro services and how they relate to the desired goal including the availability of dependencies. With context fixed to a certain domain, the engineering team will have the responsibility to take steps to improve availability.

On the other hand, in the control-based model, an engineering team will be aware of the microservices availability target, but if they fail to achieve the target there might be some punitive action. These actions may involve their ability to push the code to production. It is always better to share context on microservices availability rather than working with teams when availability has to be improved. The challenge is to provide sufficient context to teams. Whenever a non-ideal decision is made at the operations, the first query is, did the person have enough context to make a better decision?

In a big company, it is difficult to provide sufficient context so that based on the context alone the personnel can achieve the targets of their service. In these large organizations, you may have to fall back on lots of processes to reach availability goals. However, there are some cases for the control-based models. Such as in the case where lives are at stake such as in case if someone is writing unsafe software for the autopilot system of an airplane. It is up to the SRE team to decide how much risk they can take in selecting one factor out of control versus context-based models.

2. Building SRE Team

The teams are built to achieve certain objectives, and they could be winning games, launching a product, or implementing a vision. Irrespective of the field we choose, the result must be the same. There are some ways you can take to build a high performing SRE team, although building a team of high performers is a difficult task. The objective of building such a team is to reach a certain degree of operational excellence. You need to build a team that takes care of performance, availability, change management, monitoring, and emergency response and plan the services.

SRE was Google's answer to system admin Operations. The thought process they used for this was, as we are doing software development well, why we can't adopt the same practices to run the Operations section as well? And it turned out to be a very successful though. Google saw both Dev and Ops teams on the same side. They understood the targets and objectives very well and as a result, were able to make good decisions as the features were released. The main difference was how the company was structured. If the Devs and Ops were paid for competing goals, then they will not work together well as a team. Operation is an area of stability and the people are compensated for things such as availability and uptime. Devs, on the other hand, are rewarded for feature releases, which may contradict with the operations team by lowering availability.

Google was one of the first companies to realize this. Rather than placing two teams on the opposite side of the process, better results can be obtained by having them share a common goal of releasing features with reliability. DevOps and SREs are all different people assembled together for attaining a common objective. There is no fixed definition for going about things. You are required to come up with your own principles as you go along, depending on the setup.

3. Using Incident Metrics to Improve SRE at Scale

It doesn't matter whether you are looking to add a dozen users next or a million users, you are going to end up in a discussion about which areas to invest in and where to stay reliable as the services scale up. Let's look at a case study by using incident metrics to stay focused on investments. Microsoft Azure worked on the lessons that were learned while working on the service reliability ranging from startups to enterprise level to cloud scale.

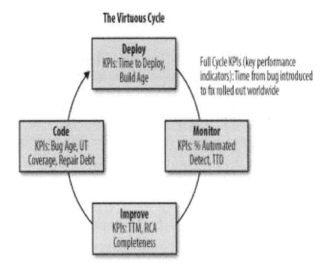

a. The Virtuous Cycle

The SRE team began by looking at the data similar to any other issue resolving effort. However, when it was attempted, it turned out that there were thousands of data sources, incident management metrics, service telemetry, and deployment metrics, and so on. It made things tricky as it had to be decided which data to look at and in what order. After consulting the experts and after looking at the best available practices, the SRE team landed on a system called The Virtuous Cycle. It created a framework which allowed the SRE team to see how useful monitoring was by finding out how fast the team detected the outages. It also depended on measuring the root-cause analysis process, repairs, and how quickly the issues were getting fixed. Then the team looked at the code quality and speed of deployment to see how quickly they would run through the full cycle.

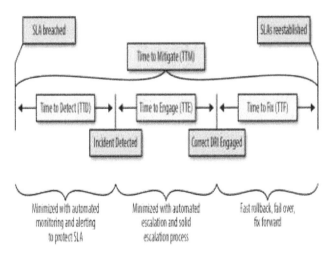

The SRE team was fully aware of how much downtime matters, so they began looking at the key metrics. They told the team how effective they were to responding to incidents and fixing them. It also meant that first, they had to define metrics that were representative of the information needed. Then agree upon definitions and timings. You could have different definitions or metrics but the group must agree on common measures and taxonomy. Agreement on taxonomy was particularly important as there might have been disconnects otherwise.

b. Metrics Review

After all these metrics were defined, the key SREs were called to look at the significant metrics that were identified as crucial to drive the virtuous cycle. Then the team tracked how they were progressing and created action plans in areas they were hitting targets. After agreeing on the metrics, the team started collecting data on how they were doing and found areas and common areas for improvement and measured the impact made by the improvements later.

The next figure shows an example of the dashboard to measure deployment and incident metrics. It allowed the team to track the trend for incident response cycle and engineer improvements in the same way as features are engineered in the product. All the incident response metrics discussed earlier show up in the figure. They measure against the targets we set and agreed on with the service owners. In case the data was found to be too much with high variability or had too many outliers, the team applied percentile to it to normalize it enough. The outliers made it easier to understand and drive the percentile close to 100%.

	Period 1	Period 2	Period 3	Period 4	Period 5	Period 6	Trend	Goal
Σ Incidents	XX	XX	XX	XX	XX	XX,XXX%		
Σ Major Incidents	X	X	X	X	X	X		
SLO	XX.XXX%	XX.XXX%	XX.XXX%	XX.XXX%	XX.XXX%	XX.XXX%		XX.XX%
TTD @ XX%ile	XX	XX	XX	XX	XX	XX		<X max
TTE @ XX%ile	XX	XX	XX	XX	XX	XX		<XX min
TTF @ XX%ile	XX	XXX	XX	XXX	XX	XX		<XX min
TTM @ XX%ile	XX	XXX	XX	XXX	XX	XX		<XX min
% Outages auto detected	XX%	XX%	XX%	XX%	XX%	XX%		X%
# SMEs engaged per ?ndgs	XX	X	XX	X	X	XX		X
DRI Hops	X	X	X	X	X	X		X

Top Incidents		Cause	TTD (mins)	TTM (mins)	Repair Items	Impact (reported)	Impact (Actual)
Incident in North Europe due to Code Bug		Code Bug	XX	XX	X	X	XXX Accounts impacted
Network Incident due to Configuration		Config	X	XX	X	X	X,XXX Accounts impacted

Deployment	XX% of clusters		XX% of clusters	
	Build Age	Build Age Trend	Build Age	Build Age Trend
Service X	XX		XXX	
Service X	XX		XX	

In the SRE metrics dashboard, there are many surrogate metrics such as DRI hops, which indicate how many on-call engineers are necessary to solve an incident. Auto-detection gives you the figures for the incidents that are detected via monitoring. These are more actionable than the top level metrics but

214

don't indicate success by themselves.

c. Repair Debt

A lot of insight that was derived out of the metrics review was available from post-incident review procedure. Every time a team member identifies a bug for repair it is logged. Repair items are fixed later, which prevents an outage from happening or reduces its duration. They are divided into short-term items or long-term items. The short-term items are rolled out faster within a week and they might be a script, a process, or even a hotfix. The long-term objects are more lasting fixes such as thorough code fixes and create broader process change. The repair items are tracked in the same management system used for tracking work management. However, what is significant is that they are logged, reportable, and distinguishable in the product backlog. Repair item tracking allows us to incorporate an operational debt in the engineering procedure and treat it like feature work.

d. Real-Time Dashboards

Probably the most significant part of a metrics review is to bring the insights and metrics into real-time dashboards. If you look at the data weekly or monthly it doesn't help to drive the changes quick enough. All the services and components need to be seen and evaluated in real time where they are working, where they are performing well, and where they could improve. Dashboards have to be created which can be pivoted by a service or a manager even down to an engineer that owns the item.

Conclusion

In a nutshell, you need to measure everything, be curious, and do not be afraid to get your hands dirty and dip into the data to find the right things to do. In many cases getting these insights needed a lot of data to be hand curated but the team understood which metrics mattered and they could automate and instrument them to help bring visibility to the metrics and help services to get better.

4. SREs Working with Third Parties

No app can be completed without third parties. Most IT professionals find them a pain to deal with but lovely for their business, and they are fantastic for marketing. None of the companies knows exactly how many 3rd party applications they have and what their value addition is. They are also not aware of the harm they could do to the performance, functionality, or security of the app. Developers are constantly challenged to add code and yet ensure that they don't break anything or start security holes and keep the app functional at all times.

5. From SysAdmin to SRE

The classical role of a system admin is defined generically as IT operations staff which is responsible for building, designing, and maintaining a company's computer infrastructure. The IT world is growing and changing constantly, and the role of SysAdmin is getting limited to hosting platforms and he can do it easily by applying policy around the server instance. Businesses are constantly changing these days and more and more of them are going towards Lean methodologies to achieve the efficiency they desire. The next stages of tech development mean the server administration gets tougher for manual operators and the infrastructure is delivered by a coded workflow. In such a case, you need to hire people who write the code. This is where SREs come in. These engineers know about data structures and programming languages along with algorithms. They can review the performance properly along with instrumenting and measuring it while running. Along with the software skills they have the know-how of the operational management, which ensures that the software has given capabilities throughout its operational life. These include resistance to failure, server, and site, scalability that can accommodate changing workloads and security patch management.

Several sysadmins have come into practice, having evolved from different sources such as help desk, support, or even just running computer systems at home. However, this evolutionary path will not work for the transition from sysadmin to SRE. The main reason for this is that the SRE require software skills and to understand the application itself, and you need to have learned these skills in a structured way. Learning programming at any level is a good starting point and the more you look at programming, the more you start to understand the developer's viewpoints. Several businesses in this world are on a journey of evolution and only a handful of them need SREs now. But all infrastructures will benefit from the fact that their sysadmin has software skills. All sysadmins need to follow this path.

6. DevOps vs. Site Reliability Engineering

As technology evolves, so too do the new roles in organizations and the level of expertise. There are two terms which have become buzzwords thanks mainly to Google branding, and they are Site Reliability Engineers and DevOps. The question is, do the responsibilities considered under the titles represent anything new or modern? Is there any real value to these roles or are they just buzzwords to further resumes?

There is enough contradiction about the titles as it is, and it has opened a debate on what their functions are and what is the difference among them. There are some people who take a hard look at the roles and come up with the summary that they are basically the same thing. Well, there is a lot in common, especially when you consider the undermining objectives such as automation, scaling, bridging the gap between development, and operations. However, there is a clear difference between them.

There are dynamic companies who wish to scale at an aggressive speed who will look to lay a foundation for an IT department which is supple and agile. To do this they will need engineering departments that can create foundations for supporting the targets. The directors of these teams will need to leverage the automation tools to enable widespread conducting of infrastructure and management to several teams. There are two main branches here to perform this. One is SRE which is clearly defined to create a fully automated IT infrastructure. The DevOps, on the other hand, is more an orchestration of a Lean or Agile development team. They serve infrastructure as the code to the programmers when required.

The IT infrastructure is pretty often built piece by piece as the organization grows. The systems are built to serve company objectives from day one. Changes will be made later as they are required. Sysadmin plays a critical role in ensuring that the daily maintenance and system updates are created to protect the investments and keep a productive environment. The admins spend their day ensuring that everything is working correctly in the company. They also ensure that everything is updated and the address breaks are there when required.

There are more sophisticated IT teams which can engineer automation scripts in the infrastructure from the beginning, removing future reliance on admin. The system architect or engineer can orchestrate patches, policy, and management over the whole network via a single CMS (Centralized Management System). These systems monitor the environment proactively and detect potential anomalies within the infrastructure before they become anomalies.

SREs are more focused on the system architect's role in core infrastructure. This is more linked to the production environment. DevOps are more related to automation and simplification of development teams and their non-production environments. The major difference between an SRE and DevOps is that the focus is on coding and the kind of environment you are placed in. DevOps will always be on the creation and testing side as they are dynamic departments and use the Lean or Agile methodology to run their operations. Also, there must be automation to help manage the processes.

Developers use automation tools such as Chef or Puppet to help with the challenges. DevOps share some common factors with SRE as well. The DevOps engineer is at the top of the pyramid architecting both a system and a culture to automate the delivery of infrastructure or other work in the development process. The main theme here is that both these new roles that are SRE and DevOps are being used to help the service run more efficiently. As we move forward, we typically expect the practices to evolve and new roles will be created. What is significant is that what drives the change is operationally efficient and is fully contingent. These forms help in supporting innovation with better speed and also aid the departments to run and scale more fluidly as a whole.

7. Production Engineering at Facebook

The production engineering lifecycle at Facebook is how they build, run, and disband their great reliability-focused teams along with performance, scalability, and efficiency. It was started in 2009 with a handful of engineers in a single office. Now there are several hundreds of engineers that support dozens of teams in four countries and 6 offices. When Facebook production engineers are hired they have to be good coders in at least one shell language. They need to know TCP/IP Networking, Linux Systems, Distributed systems design, and debugging, reliability engineering background and be available on call.

5. SRE Processes and Best Practices

In simple terms, SREs run services by using a set of networked systems, operated for users that might be internal and external. They are also responsible for the wellbeing of these services. Operating a service successfully means a wide range of activities, such as planning capability, monitoring, responding to incidents, making sure that the root causes for the outages are systematically addressed, etc.

SREs represent a break away from the current industry best practices for managing difficult and large services. The SRE was originally influenced by software engineering, but now SRE methodologies have become a different set of principles, practices, and a set of incentives in the field of DevOps area of expertise.

Some key SRE nest practices are:

- Support the services before they

are live via activities like developing software frameworks and platforms, system design consulting, launch reviews, and capacity planning.

- Engaging in improving the complete life cycle of services. This means from inception and design stage to deployment, operations, and refinement.

- Maintenance of services when they are live by monitoring and measuring the availability, latency, and overall health of the system.

- Practising incident response that is sustainable and quality postmortems.

- Scaling of systems via mechanisms such as automation, and evolution of systems by pushing the necessary changes to improve speed and reliability.

The networking technology addresses several challenges that are associated with SREs and their best practices. In order to ensure optimum network performance and network operations, the SRE team needs a detailed and correct application and networking insight to ensure system performance and availability.

1. Handling Overload

Avoiding the overload condition is the target for load balancing policies. However, no matter how good your load balancing policy is, eventually some parts of the system become overloaded. Handling overload conditions gracefully is a fundamental requirement in running any reliable serving system. It is also important that individual tasks are also protected against overload conditions. For example, a backend task serving a certain traffic rate should continue to keep doing so at the same rate without any impact on the latency. This needs to continue despite how much surplus traffic is added at the task.

The backend chore should not fall over and crash while placed under the load. The statements must hold true for a definite rate of traffic which is 2X or even 10X of what the task is allotted to process. It is an accepted fact that at a certain point the system will break down and raising the point at which the breakdown occurs is very difficult to achieve.

The key to handling overload conditions is to take degradation conditions seriously. If the situations are ignored, various systems display terrible behaviour. As work piles up the tasks find it hard to run and they ultimately run out of retention and crash or even might end up burning the CPU. Latency suffers pretty badly as the traffic is dropping and the tasks start competing for resources. If the condition is left unchecked a failure in a subgroup of a system can trigger multiple failures in other system components causing the entire system to fail at some point in time. The impact from this can be so damaging that it is dangerous for any scheme operating at scale to have protection against it.

It is a common misconception that the overloaded backend must turn down and halt accepting all the traffic. This conception goes against the target of robust load balancing. It is better for the backend to keep accepting as much circulation as possible but only accept the load as the memory frees up. A quality backend, if supported by strong load balancing strategies, will accept only those requests it can process gracefully and reject the others.

There is a range of tools available for implementing quality load balancing and overload protection. But they are not magic, as load balancing needs a thorough understanding of systems and the semantics of the requests. There are many techniques used by Google that have evolved and will continue to do so as the nature of systems continues to modify.

2. SRE Engagement Model Evolution

We have discussed so far what happens when the SRE is already in place and in custody of a service. But very few facilities begin their lifespan enjoying SRE support. Therefore, there is a need to have a process for assessing a service, ensuring that it needs the support of an SRE, a negotiation about how to improve the negative conditions that block SRE support and really have the SREs. This process is called onboarding. In case you are in a situation where you are bounded by many services which are in a different state of completion and excellence, your SRE team is probably running through an ordered queue for onboardings for quite some time. It would have finished taking on the high-value targets by now.

This is a common and totally reasonable method of dealing with such a fait accompli situation. However, there are at least two different ways of bringing in the wisdom gathered from production and SRE care to the services new and old. In the first scenario like software engineering, the earlier an SRE team is consulted the better. It is similar to finding a bug early. The earlier it is found, the cheaper it is to repair it. The earlier an SRE team is consulted the more beneficial it will be. When SREs are engaged early in the stages of design the onboarding time is lowered and the services become more reliable. This is normally because there is no reason to unwind suboptimal design or its implementation.

The second way is perhaps the best way and it involves short-circuiting the process due to which specially fashioned systems having a lot of individual differences end up at the SRE door. Provide the PD team with a platform that is validated by the SRE infrastructure upon which the production team can build their system. The platform will benefit both reliability and scalability. This also avoids some cognitive load issues completely and by addressing the general infrastructure

231

practices it allows the product development team to focus on innovations at the application layer stage where it belongs.

It is certain that service reliability can be improved by SRE engagement. It is a process in which there are systematic reviews and improvement of the production process. The SREs initial such approach in Google was Simple Production Readiness Review that went a long way in standardizing the SRE engagement model, but it was applicable only to services that had reached the launching phase. Over a period of time, SREs extended and improved this model.

The earlier engagement model showed SRE involving in the development life cycle earlier as it improved the design for reliability. The demand for SRE expertise has grown since then and a more scalable model is envisaged. Some frameworks were developed for production services to meet this demand. Codes based on the best practices of production were standardized and encapsulated in the framework. So this meant that use of frameworks was recommended, simple, consistent way of building production enables services. Adoption of the framework has become a prominent influence on developing Google's production ready services. They were also responsible for expanding SRE contribution lowering the overheads such as service management and thereby improving the baseline service quality of the company.

3. Accelerating the SREs to On-Call and More than That

The trick is to speed up the newbies and at the same time keep the senior SREs up to speed in the process. So, you have hired your set of SREs but now what? Now you need to train them on the work. You need to invest upfront in their education and technical orientation that will hopefully make them better engineers. This kind of training makes them proficient by accelerating their training process. It also makes their skills more balanced, sharp and robust.

The most successful SRE teams are built through mutual trust. In order to maintain any service consistently and universally, you are required to trust fellow colleagues to know the system. Not only are they required to know the system, but they must also be able to diagnose system behaviour and they should be available for help easily. They must also react under pressure for saving your day. so SRE education doesn't end at, "What does a newcomer need to learn to be on-call?" Given the requirements of trust, you are also needed to ask questions such as:

- How many current co-workers are assessing the readiness of a newcomer for the on-call role?

- How can we incorporate the enthusiasm and curiosity in the newbies to ensure that the existing SREs benefit from them?

- What are the activities to get the team involved to benefit everyone in terms of their education? Everyone must enjoy the process.

All students have a range of learning preferences. Learning that you will have to hire people who have a mix of these preferences. You will choose someone with one kind of style ignoring another set of expenses. There is no fixed style of education to train new SREs and there is certainly no magic formula that works for the entire SRE team. Below there are some recommended training practices that are well known at the SRE of Google? These represent a huge range of options available to make your team an expert in the SRE concepts, both now and on an ongoing basis.

Here are some recommended patterns,

- Design sequential and concrete learning material/experiences for students. Deluge students off their menial work.

- Encourage statistical thinking, reverse engineering, fundamental, and working principles. Avoid training them strictly through operational procedures, playbooks, and checklists.

- Encourage students to read the failure analysis by suggesting postmortems. Avoid efforts to bury the outages to conceal the blame.

- Create realistic breakages allowing students to fix them with real monitoring and tooling. This avoids students from having the first chance to fix when he is already on-call.

- Encourage role playing with theoretical disasters as a group to improve a team's issue solving ability. Avoid experts being created who are compartmentalized.

- Allow students to shadow on-call

rotations early, thereby allowing them to compare notes with the on-caller. Avoids students from getting to the on-call situation before their knowledge is holistic.

- Pair the student with expert SREs to be able to revise on-call training plans. This stops the thinking that the incident is to be touched by experts only.

- Allow the students partial ownership by giving them nontrivial project work. This nullifies the tendency for the expert to get significant work and the newbie's left cleaning up the scraps.

4. Dealing with Interrupts

The operational load is the work when applied to complex systems must be done in order to maintain a system in a functional state. Viz. in case you own a car, someone will always service it, place gas in it, or do other maintenance work related to it to keep it performing its functionalities. All complex systems are as full of errors as its creators.

There are many forms of operational overloads when they are applied to maintaining complex systems. Some of them are more obvious than others. The terminology used may change but the operational load falls under three categories: tickets, pages, and ongoing operational activities.

Pages: They are related to production alerts and their fallouts. Pages are triggered in response to production emergencies. They are many times recurring and monotonous, needing little thought. They may also be involving and with in-depth tactical thought. These pages have an SLO (expected response time) that is measured in minutes.

Tickets: Tickets are customer requests that ask you to take action. Like pages, tickets may be boring and simple or may need real thinking. One simple ticket may request a code review for a configuration that the team owns or a more complex ticket may entail special requests for help with a decision or capacity plans. Tickets can also have SLO, but in this case, the response time is measured in hours, days, and weeks.

Ongoing Operational Responsibilities: They are also referred to as "Kicking the can down the road" or "Toil". They involve activities such as team owned code or flag rollouts, or responses to sudden situations or time-sensitive queries from clients. Although they do not have a definite SLO these tasks may interrupt you.

There are operational overloads that can be anticipated easily or planned for but most of them are unplanned. It can interrupt someone at any non-specific time requiring the person to make a decision whether it can wait or not.

5. Recovering an SRE from Operational Overload

It is a common policy for the Google SRE team to evenly divide their time between their developments and sensitive ops work. Their balance remains upset for several months due to a surge in daily tickets volume. A massive amount of ops work is particularly dangerous as the SRE team may burn out or become handicapped to make progress on the project at hand. Whenever a team must allocate an uneven amount of time to resolve tickets at the cost of spending time on improving service, its reliability, and scalability suffer.

One way of relieving this burden is by temporarily transferring an additional SRE in the overloaded team. Once this person is embedded in the team, the SRE focuses on improving practices opposed to just helping the team empty the ticket queue. This SRE observes the daily routine of the team and recommends certain points to improve team practices. This adds a fresh perspective to the team performance and their routines that cannot be provided by the team itself.

However, while using this approach, it is necessary to transfer more than a single engineer. Well, two SREs does not necessarily mean better results. It may cause issues in case the team doesn't react suitably to them.

6. Communicating and Collaboration within SRE

The SRE organizational position in Google is stimulating and has a clear effect on how you communicate and collaborate. There is a huge diversity involved in SRE work and how it is done. There are service teams, infrastructure teams, and horizontal product teams. There are relationships involved with product growth teams sometimes much larger than SRE teams and sometimes the same size. Then there are situations in which the SRE team is the product development team. SRE teams are made from people who are equipped with architectural skills or system engineering skills, project management skills, software engineering skills, leadership qualities, and a background in all fields of engineering. They do not have just a single model and they have more than one configuration that works. This flexibility is suitable for their ultimate pragmatic nature.

It is also a fact that the SRE is not your command and control company. Normally they have an alliance with at least two masters, one for service and the other for infrastructure. They work in general SRE context. The relationship with service is very strong as they are held responsible for the show of those systems. However, despite that relationship, the actual reporting lines are via SRE as a whole. Nowadays, the SRE spends more time supporting their independent services across the production work. But they come from shared values culture and, as a result, they have a strong homogeneous approach to the issues. It is so by design.

The facts mentioned above have steered SRE organizations in certain directions whilst taking into consideration two crucial dimensions called communication and collaboration. For communication, the apt computing metaphor will be data flow. Similar to the fact that data must flow around the production, it has to flow around SRE as well. Data could be about the condition of the services, projects, production, and the condition of the persons. For the highest efficiency of a team, service data must move in a reliable way from one point to another. One way of thinking about this flow is by thinking about the interface an SRE team must show to other teams like the APL. Like the APL a good design is critical for the effective operation, and in case the API is incorrect it will be very difficult to correct later on.

The API is also pertinent for collaboration as contract metaphor both for the SRE teams and between product development and SRE teams. They all need to progress in an environment with constant change. This collaboration looks pretty much like a collaboration between any other fast-moving organization. The only difference being the mix of system engineering expertise, software engineering skills, and the wisdom gathered out of production that the SRE brings to the collaboration. The best design and best implementation happen when there is a joint concern between production and the invention being met with mutual respect. This happens to be the promise an SRE makes to an organization. They are equipped with dependability, with similar skills as that of product development teams. This improves things a great deal. Experience indicates that just having a person in charge of consistency without the full skill set will not be enough for the job.

Considering the globally spread nature of SRE teams, effective communication will always be a high priority within the SRE. The collaboration within the SRE teams has its challenges but also great rewards, including a common approach to the platform for solving issues and allowing the team to focus on more difficult issues.

7. Testing for Reliability

One of the key responsibilities of SREs is to quantify the confidence in the system they are maintaining. This is achieved by SREs adapting the classical software testing techniques at scale to the systems. The confidence can be measured in terms of past reliability and forthcoming reliability. Past is captured by analyzing the data provided via monitoring the system behaviour. While the future is quantified by making educated predictions from the data indicated in the past system behaviour. To make sure that these predictions are correct to be of use, one of the subsequent conditions must be good:

- The website has remained totally unchanged over a period of time without any software publications or changes in servers. This means that the future behaviour of the system will be the same as the past.

- You can confidently tell all changes to the website with the analysis which will follow indicate all uncertainties incurred due to the changes.

Testing is a method used to establish specific areas of similarity when there are changes. Every test that passes before and after the changes reduces the uncertainty factor for which the analysis follows. Thorough testing allows us to predict the reliability of a system with sufficient details to be pragmatically useful. The amount of testing required hinges on the reliability requirements of the system.

As the percentile of codebase covered by tests increases, you are reducing the uncertainty and increase the reliability in the system. Sufficient testing means that you are permitted to make more changes before the reliability falls below a certain acceptable level. In case you make too many changes too fast. the reliability also approaches the acceptability mark quickly. You should stop making any changes at this point while the new data accumulates. This accumulated data supplements the test coverage and validates the reliability asserted for the revised paths of execution. By assuming that the served clients are arbitrarily distributed, the sampling statistics are more reliable. They are extrapolated from the monitored metrics and the aggregate behaviour indicates the use of new paths. The statistics identify certain areas that need heavier testing.

8. Software Engineering within SRE

In case you ask someone to title any Google software engineering work, they are likely to name one of the consumer-facing products such as Google Maps or Gmail. Some people may mention the underlying infrastructures such as Colossus or Bigtable. However, the truth is that there is an enormous amount of software engineering that goes on behind the scenes that the consumers never get to see and many of those yields are prepared within SRE.

Google has a production environment which by some way is one of the utmost complex ones that humanity has ever developed. SREs have readymade experience with the nitty-gritty of production. That makes them exceptionally well suited to make the suitable tools required to solve internal issues and use the cases that are related to keeping the production running. The bulk of the tools are connected to the overall objective of maintaining the uptime and keeping the latency low and assume many forms. Examples of this are monitoring binary rollout mechanisms, or a development setting built on a dynamic server composition.

All-in-all these tools developed by SRE are developed software engineering projects and are different from unique solutions and quick hacks. The SREs that have developed these products have adopted a mindset that is a product based that considers both the internal customers and the roadmap for future plans.

In several ways, the huge measure of Google production has demanded internal software development. This is mainly because very few third-party tools must be developed at the necessary scale for Google's needs. Google's history of successful projects in software engineering has led many to agree to the doles of developing straight within the SRE. SREs are in a good position to develop this internal software for several reasons.

The software engineering projects in Google SRE have grown with the organization and, in several cases, the lessons that were learned from the successful execution of earlier development projects have paved the way for their subsequent endeavours. The unique and hands-on experience that SREs have brought to the development tools leads to innovative approaches to conventional issues. The SRE driven projects are clearly beneficial to the organization in creating a successful model for supporting the services at scale. As SREs often develop software to streamline the inefficient processes or automate common tasks. The projects mean that the SRE teams do not have to scale linearly with the size of the services they are supporting. In the end, the benefits of having the SRE devoting some of their time to software development are always reaped by the organization.

9. Load Balancing at the Front End/in the Datacenter

Google serves several million requirements every second at the front end. Obviously, they use more than just a single computer for handling all these requests. However, even if there was a single supercomputer that was someway able to handle all the requirements at the same time, Google will still not employ a policy that relies on a single point failure. When you are dealing with systems that are so big, placing all your eggs in a single basket is a sure recipe for disaster. Now let us consider load balancing within the datacenter. Application level policies are used for routing the requests onto individual servers which can process them.

10. Managing a Critical State

It is a reality that processes crash or needs to be resumed. Hard drives also fail. Natural disasters are responsible for taking out many datacenters in a region. SREs are required to anticipate these kinds of disasters and develop strategies which will run the service despite calamities. The strategies usually mean running these systems on several websites. Distributing a system geographically is relatively straightforward but it involves maintaining a consistent view of the state of the system which is indeed difficult and a nuanced undertaking. There are groups of processes which may wish to agree reliably on the following queries:

- Which is the leader of the group process?

- What is the state of processes

involved in a group?

- Does the process hold lease?

- Has the message been committed successfully to distribute queues?

- What is the given key's value in a data store?

Distributed consensus is very effective in building highly available and reliable systems that need a constant view of some state of the system. The distributed consensus means reaching an agreement amongst a collection of processes linked by an unreliable network. For example, many processes in a scattered system are needed to form a constant view of a critical configuration. This is despite whether the distributed lock is seized or the message in the queue is processed or not.

Keep in mind the kind of problems the distributed consensus can be used to solve. Also, remember the kinds of problems that can arise when ad hoc methods like heartbeats are utilized instead of the distributed consensus. When you see the critical shared state, leader election, or distributed locking always think of distributed consensus. Any lesser approach will be a ticking bomb waiting to explode in the system.

6. Building SRE Success Culture at LinkedIn (A Case Study)

Being an SRE (Site Reliability Engineer) means having to face a lot of tough problems. Complex failure scenarios, outages, and other technical crises are amongst the things they must be ready to deal with every working day at LinkedIn. When they are not dealing with problems they are discussing them. They perform regular postmortems and root cause analysis and they are required to dig into difficult technical difficulties in an unflinching and relentless way.

Strangely enough, discussing culture in an SRE association can be a lot harder. At LinkedIn, it is constantly discussed how the culture is equally as important as their products. And yet it is tough to have a blueprint for other teams and companies to aid them in creating the right SRE culture. One wishes there were easy steps to follow in the technology industry. Things like range and inclusion are common in the tech world. As things are, there are several companies looking to generate a positive culture but are not always sure how to go on board the process.

1. A postmortem on the SRE Culture at LinkedIn

They are certainly not claiming that they have found a formula that fit all the processes for creating the correct engineering culture. But two engineers from the team told their boss that they feel the LinkedIn culture is exclusive and as an employee they felt valued and supported despite their backgrounds.

This caused the writer to reflect on SRE organization culture specifically because he knew that things were not like that always. He has mentioned below some changes they made over the years for installing an all-inclusive culture, a positive attitude, and discussion of activities performed on a daily basis. And to maintain the procedures.

255

Although this is not a specific guide some of the thoughts and their experiences are sure to benefit those looking to change the organizational culture.

2. Fighting Fire in the Early Years

In the earlier years of the SRE team, they were not even called SREs. Their role was more of a mixture of firefighting, release management, and conventional operations. The focus was completely on getting these things done and there was no culture to speak of. Now, the LinkedIn site was infused with many reliability issues as it was faced with hyper growth. All the tech team could think of was to keep things going. There was no time to think of the culture they were creating, technically or otherwise.

When things finally levelled up a little, they decided that they needed to make grave changes to the team to correct the various issues with the product. They reorganized themselves as an SRE team and tasked themselves with a clear goal in mind and that was to keep the website up and running all the time. In order to align with this assignment, they decided to embrace values of ownership and craftsmanship across engineering. This meant they felt totally responsible for the site like they were the owners of it. They viewed their functions as a craft, which requires execution.

This overhaul to an extent was successful. The site was moved into a more stable position and the role of the operations team to solve the issues was made via software instead of people and process.

3. Dealing with the Culture Debt

Like all the SREs, the LinkedIn team SREs are always thinking about things such as efficiency, resilience, automation, and the availability of team member experience. When you are tackling these issues every day you are working with other teams or other SREs in a larger engineering organization. So we need SREs that are aware of the importance of collaboration with other people.

As the LinkedIn technical situation was terrible during their hyper-growth period, they have come to value their technical skills above all in their management and hiring processes. Rather than considering whether candidates will be people that will be great teammates in the long-run, they placed more importance on their technical capabilities and how they could help in the short-term. Although this got them some very talented individuals it also revealed certain flaws over a period. Having engineers who not exactly great team players were made collaborative work more difficult. The work is a vital part of site reliability. In many cases, it created a negative work atmosphere. After a while, the experience became so painful for everyone involved that a need for change was observed. This was similar to how a technical debt builds up in a long-lived code base. Over a period they made specific changes to their philosophy, people, and their processes in the SRE. This is how they solved the cultural debt that was built over time.

4. Philosophy

The head of engineering and operations at LinkedIn was David Hanke, who began promoting the SREs to have a mindset of attacking the problem and not the person involved. The SRE team's daily work is to constantly identify and correct issues and bugs. So it is vital to remember that we are all on the same team and are fighting against outages. It fostered a culture of equality and inclusion in the SRE team's mindset. So, whenever there was an outage, it was not considered as my problem, but our problem and we are all together to fix it.

5. People

In 2013 LinkedIn invested plenty of effort into formalizing and evolving their SREs interview process. Part of the process was explicitly looking for the missing collaborative spirit they wished their engineers displayed. This was of course in addition to technical abilities. Slowly this began to build their ranks with people who fit this culture as they were not just equipped technically but became a part of the culture. By the time this level of maturity was reached in the hiring process, there were around 100 people in the SRE team. It was a far cry from that handful of people that started out in the earlier years. As the organization grew the ability to collaborate successfully became more tied directly to technical work. Not focusing on the quality of new hires only functioned for a while, as they were a smaller company.

6. Process

Nowadays the LinkedIn SRE team consists of hundreds of SRE engineers located in different geographic locations. To have scaling culture along with a team is challenging, but what really helps them a great deal is that their leadership is aligned towards the environment they wish to create. Everyone knows the significance of having a cooperative and all-inclusive culture and so it is their priority to preserve it. Part of it is by reinforcing the values in the daily stand up meeting.

Each day, the SRE goes along with anybody who wishes to participate in a short conference or go over website reliability issues from the past 24 hours and the immediate preventive fixes that are being implemented for every incident. As these topics are being discussed, they ensure that a solution is approached not only from a technical standpoint but from a cultural point of view. For example, if a defensive behaviour is observed, they will tell the team to attack the issue and not the person. Or, in case an outage was because of a breakdown in communication, time is taken to re-emphasize that they are all on an identical team and need to see each other in the same light.

One part of these conferences is that the culture is not made a separate aspect on its own. It is always integrated in the way the problems of the day, such as recurring bugs or site outages, are discussed. As a result, you are doing your job correctly from the technical perspective and are following cultural values as well. The two are moving ahead healthily as they are intertwined.

7. Conclusion

They don't make-believe to be perfect and understand that there is still a lot of work to be done. But hearing fellow SREs say that they are treated well and with equality makes the manager feel that they are moving in the right direction. These examples, such as hiring for cultural fitting or making cultural and procedural values consistent and reinforcing these standards daily, can help create a culture you want to see in an organization.

7. SRE & DevOps: Similarities & Differences

So, how is it going? Though I have passed on useful information regarding SRE Principles, Processes, Implementation and case studies, there is one important topic I wanted to cover. There are many views and definitions of the similarities and differences of DevOps and SRE.Lets collate them and see how it shapes up!

So, while taking the SRE and DevOps names in one go, this is what the subject matter experts are saying about both of them!

1. About DevOps:

- The core reason for the DevOps movement to start was the lack of production exposure of coders. They were writing codes without any idea of what the other guy in the production environment goes through.

- DevOps is more of an organizational culture which fills the gap between coder and the operation person and aligns them to the overall organizational goal.

- Overall DevOps culture is an abstract class which leaves the implementation details to be customized by the author.

2. About SRE:

- SRE is what happens when a software engineer is entrusted with operations!

- SRE was developed by Google for internal consumption and overlaps with the DevOps culture and philosophy. But, the SRE is more explicit and measures and achieves reliability. Overall, SRE advice the way forward *to achieve reliability and success in various DevOps areas.*

3. Differences

- The major difference in the problem-solving approach is that DevOps team raises the problem and sends it to Dev to solve, whereas the SRE team take the ownership of solving it too.

- SRE team is more confident in handling the production environment where a DevOps team doesn't interfere often with the production. Also, improving operational efficiency and performance is one of the goals of an SRE.

- SRE is an approach where the coders are given the ownership to deploy, monitor and maintain the application releases. SRE philosophy believes in taking charge and deploying developers who have an operations mindset, whereas DevOps believes in the bridge the dev and op gap by aligning the goals of the teams with that of the organization.

4. Is it bird, plane or Superman! Are we doing DevOps or SRE?

- According to many companies that implemented SRE in a slightly different way than Google, you don't have to decide. At Reddit, ops engineers work on reducing toil, improving deployment and scaling processes, but they are referred to as "DevOps."

- One more example can be taken of Logz.io which defined the role as DevOps and not SRE: "They fill the gap between coders and operations through automated monitoring and performance stress- testing".

5. Similarities

Both SRE and DevOps are aiming for:

- Monitor and Measure the success

- Move from Silos to collaboration between Dev & Ops Teams

- Move towards Organizational Culture more accepting of failures

- Automation

6. DevOps Pillars vs. SRE Practices

DevOps	SRE
Measure	availability, uptime, outages, toil, etc. is measured
Reduce Silos	Same tools & techniques are used by developers and ops

Accept Failure	The formula for containing & balancing failures in new releases
Automation	Minimizing manual work for long term value addition
Gradual Change	Do fail and move ahead quickly to reduce the cost of failure

Conclusion

As the SRE industry has grown, there are a couple of different dynamics that have come into play. First, are the consistent primary responsibilities of the SRE and the concerns over a period of time. Systems might be 1000 times faster or larger but the real need is for them to remain reliable, easy to manage in case of emergencies, and flexible. They also need to be well monitored and have their capacities planned. At the same time, normal activities undertaken by the SREs have evolved as Google services and other company products have matured. For example, once upon a time for Google a goal was to build a single dashboard for twenty machines. Now it is an automatic discovery. Just get to dashboard building and alert a fleet of thousands of machines at a time.

An SRE team must be as compact as possible. It should operate at a great degree of abstraction in the process relying on many backup systems as fail-safes along with APIs to collaborate with the systems. The SRE team must have a solid knowledge of the systems and how they work. They must also know how they fail and how they must respond to these failures. This comes from working on those failures from day to day.

Most practices and principles used by Google for SRE are evident across a range of industries out there. The lessons learned by established industries have inspired several other practices in use today. The significance of outages can be vital to many industries. For example, people could get injured or even die if there is an outage in the case of some industries such as medical, aviation, or nuclear. When the stakes are very high there has to be a conservative approach as the reliability is of paramount importance.

If we consider an industry such as Google, there is a constant tightrope between high reliability expected by users and the sharp focus on innovation and rapid changes. Google is unbelievably serious about reliability and they create approaches for the high rate of change. Of course, in many cases, the reliability of term reliability is also taken into consideration.

** How did you like the book? Could you spare some time and review it.

My Other Books available across the platforms in e-book, paperback and audible versions:

1. BlockchainTechnology: Introduction to Blockchain Technology and its impact on Business Ecosystem

2. DevOps Handbook: Introduction to DevOps and its Impact on Business Ecosystem

3. Blockchain Technology and DevOps: Introduction and Impact on Business Ecosystem

4. **Love Yourself: a 21-day plan for learning "Self-Love" to cultivate self-worth, self-belief, self-confidence & happiness**

5. Intermittent Fasting: 7 effective techniques of Intermittent Fasting

7 EFFECTIVE TECHNIQUES OF

INTERMITTENT FASTING

Stay Healthy,Lose Weight,
Slow Down Aging Process & Live Longer!

STEPHEN FLEMING

6. Love Yourself and intermittent Fasting(Mind and Body Bundle Book)

New Releases 2018-19

280

You can check all my Books on my **Amazon's Author Page**

** If you prefer audible versions of these books, I have few free coupons, mail me at <u>valueadd2life@gmail.com</u>. If available, I would mail you the same.

Made in the USA
Las Vegas, NV
12 May 2021